The Embrace of God's Mercy

Mother Elvira Petrozzi

The EMBRACE *of* GOD'S MERCY

Mother Elvira and the Story of Community Cenacolo

As told to Michele Casella

Translated by Charlotte J. Fasi and Community Cenacolo

SOPHIA INSTITUTE PRESS
Manchester, New Hampshire

Sophia Institute Press
Box 5284, Manchester, NH 03108
1-800-888-9344
www.SophiaInstitute.com

Sophia Institute Press® is a registered trademark of Sophia Institute.

Library of Congress Cataloging-in-Publication Data
Names: Petrozzi, Elvira, 1937- author. | Casella, Michele, 1979- editor. |
Fasi, Charlotte J., translator.
Title: The embrace of God's mercy : Mother Elvira and the story of Community
Cenacolo / Mother Elvira Petrozzi ; edited by Michele Casella ;
translated by Charlotte J. Fasi.
Other titles: Abbraccio. English
Description: Manchester, New Hampshire : Sophia Institute Press, 2019. |
"The Embrace of God's Mercy is a translation of L'abbraccio : storia
della Comunità Cenacolo (Milan: Edizioni San Paolo, 2013)." | Summary:
"The story of the founding and growth of Comunità Cenacolo, a free,
fully residential Catholic program for people seeking to overcome
substance abuse, founded in Saluzzo, Italy, in 1983 by Mother Elvira
Petrozzi"— Provided by publisher.
Identifiers: LCCN 2019038121 | ISBN 9781622828326 (paperback) | ISBN
9781622828333 (epub)
Subjects: LCSH: Petrozzi, Elvira, 1937- | Comunità Cenacolo. | Substance
abuse treatment facilities—Italy—Saluzzo—History. | Substance
abuse—Treatment—Religious aspects—Catholic Church. |
Nuns—Italy—Biography.
Classification: LCC RC564.67.I8 P4813 2019 | DDC 362.290945/13—dc23
LC record available at https://lccn.loc.gov/2019038121

First printing

Contents

Foreword

This English edition of the story of the Cenacolo Community in Mother Elvira Petrozzi's own words is long overdue. The Italian version — *L'Abbraccio* — came out in 2013, and Sophia Institute Press is to be commended for making this unique story available to the English-speaking world. I am confident that it will become, before long, a spiritual classic, seen by many as one of the great spiritual commentaries of our times.

The title — *The Embrace of God's Mercy* — chosen by Mother Elvira, fittingly sums up this amazing story. People who have known her have experienced, on meeting her, a warm embrace and a wide, endearing smile. They knew, without a doubt, that they were very special to her. Everybody she meets is special to her. The story of the forgiving father welcoming back his prodigal son in Luke's Gospel (chapter 15) is an apt picture of the kind of welcome Mother Elvira gives, especially to the members of her Cenacolo family.

I met Mother Elvira more than twenty-five years ago in Rome, Italy, while in search of help for a community that was launched in St. Augustine, Florida, in the early 1990s by our local St. Vincent de Paul Society, me, and a couple of former students from the University of Florida. I had earlier pastored that university parish in Gainesville, Florida.

At St. Vincent de Paul Farm, we formed Our Lady of Hope Community for the homeless who were coming to our St. Augustine Cathedral parish, where I was then assigned as pastor, to help get them off the street. We were in a little over our heads and struggled to handle the situations of the people coming to us. It was then that I heard that the Church in Italy had success stories in this kind of endeavor.

While on a sabbatical in Rome, I met a kind priest who was an official of the Council on the Family, Monsignor Anthony LaFemina. He had been researching programs around the world for a document he would help draft on Drug Addiction and Family Life. There were a fair number of effective efforts by Catholics in Italy at the time to address the drug problem. In Italy, heroin addiction was taking the lives of many. In the United States, crack cocaine had emerged as a popular drug of choice. Monsignor LaFemina became well acquainted with people leading the charge on the drug crisis in Italy and throughout the world.

Early on, a book in Italian, *Le Droghe, Come Uscirne?* (on how to get out of the world of drugs), described some of the Italian Church leaders who assisted people struggling with drugs. Among the people cited in that book was the foundress of the Cenacolo Community, Mother Elvira.

The word *Cenacolo* is Italian for the "Cenacle," the Upper Room where the Last Supper took place. While the word can be translated as "Cenacle," most American friends of the Community refer to it as *Cenacolo*, with the initial "c" pronounced "ch," as in Italy.

Mother Elvira's story describes the founding of her community in an old, abandoned building owned by the town of Saluzzo in

Northern Italy, near Turin. The only positive element of the ramshackle building at the time was a terra-cotta image of the Blessed Mother over the entrance. That was enough for Mother Elvira to be hopeful for the future. The building itself and its reconstruction were symbolic of the resurrection of the lives, shattered by hopelessness and despair, that would occur through the efforts of the Cenacolo Community. Initially Mother Elvira had no plans other than working out of that one building. But the hand of God would direct her otherwise. Today, there are more than seventy communities worldwide.

While in Rome, my faltering attempt at Italian was enough for me to develop what has become a lifelong friendship with Mother Elvira and a deep respect for her holiness of life, a life rooted in devotion to the Lord of the Eucharist and our Blessed Mother. I regard her as one of the spiritual giants of our times, who, through her teachings and writings, is helping young people, and the old as well, to develop a profound encounter with God—helping people truly encounter the One who is the source of their happiness, and helping them to face honestly the hurdles thrown into their everyday lives, rather than try to escape from them.

Her proposal is not an easy one.

Where in the world today do you find young men and women praying the Mysteries of the Rosary three times a day? Where in the world today do you find laypeople reflecting on their lives in community regularly, in what they refer to as *Revisione della Vita* (A review of life)? Where do you find anywhere a work ethic that regards doing a job well from start to finish, in a disciplined fashion, using one's God-given talents?

Well, maybe under Coach Nick Sabin at the University of Alabama, who reminds his football team that there are two kinds of pain in the world: one caused by discipline and the other caused by disappointment. If you choose the pain of discipline, he says, you won't have to face the pain of disappointment. Mother Elvira shares that same kind of perspective. That is why she has so many success stories. As she once told me, "*Habiamo risulti, Padre*" (We have results, Father).

I would often drive west from downtown St. Augustine on Route 16 to the Cenacolo Community on a hot summer day and see no one working in the fields along the way — not until I got to Our Lady of Hope Cenacolo Community. For the members of that Community, work was not an enemy, but a friend. They may have led undisciplined lives before, but Mother Elvira helped them find motivation for their work in their faith, in the Lord of the Eucharist. People who were looking for well-trained workers knew they would find them among the disciples of Mother Elvira. Former community members would have no trouble finding a job after exiting the community.

Over twenty-five years ago, Mother Elvira accepted my invitation to send community members to the United States. But it took a while for her community to get established initially. It did not appear that American young people could handle the high bar Mother Elvira had set for her communities — in prayer, in discipline, in community life, in lifestyle, in work. The Italian-born community leader Albino Aragno and I felt it just wasn't going to work in the United States. He mentioned our opinion to Mother Elvira. Saintly woman that she was, she gave us her message and mandate: if there is one American in that house in the United States, you Italians are staying!

Well, there was one American. His name was Ben. Ben stayed … and then others came … and stayed; and still more came later and stayed.

And do you know what?

Albino and I were proven wrong. Mother Elvira knew young people, including American young people, better than we did.

American youths are up to the task. The problem is that the bar, the challenge, has been set too low for them by most of us in Church leadership. Mother Elvira knew that! She was a great visionary, a great prophet for our times!

Her Cenacolo Community is now well known by many throughout the Church. Pope Francis, as Cardinal Bergoglio, invited the Cenacolo Community to Argentina. Cardinal Schönborn welcomed her community to Austria. Mother Elvira has located many communities close to Marian shrines throughout the world. (With Catholics throughout the world, she awaits the Church's final verdict for approbation of the alleged apparitions in Medjugorje.)

Mother Elvira's meditations have appeared through the years in the popular publication *Magnificat*. *Catholic Digest* and the *National Catholic Register* have done feature articles on the Cenacolo Community. Each year on Good Friday, EWTN televises the Stations of the Cross, powerfully presented by Cenacolo members from the Shrine of the Most Blessed Sacrament in Hanceville, Alabama.

Families throughout the world, with sons and daughters in Mother Elvira's communities, have come to know her spirituality. In the United States, there are now three communities of men and one community of women (contact information on the American communities can be found at HopeReborn.org.).

Unfortunately, too few in the English-speaking world have come to know this dedicated woman of deep faith. I join many friends of the Cenacolo communities in thanking Sophia Institute Press for making available this extraordinary story, which will touch the minds and hearts of many and help them to know there is definitely hope for all, all who are willing to welcome the outstretched arms and warm "embrace" of a modern-day saint, Mother Elvira Petrozzi. In her embrace, they will indeed discover the powerful and irresistible embrace that is the love of God—Father, Son, and Holy Spirit!

—Most Rev. Robert J. Baker, S.T.D.
Bishop of Birmingham

Introduction

During the First International Apostolic Congress of Divine Mercy held in Rome in April 2008, Mother Elvira concluded her testimony with these words:

"Thank you! I am very happy to have participated at this ... at this ..."

She failed to find the word, and then one of the presenters suggested to her: "Congress!"

Mother Elvira responded, "But these are words that I never use!"

Everyone smiled, including her. Then she added:

"Please excuse me. I am a poor, really poor, *but really poor* ... I don't want to say *ignorant* ... I am a *goose*! But I'm a cheerful goose that's always happy and alive ... alive ... ALIVE!"

Her simplicity characterizes the pages of this book. Her words aren't cautiously constructed or modified, but direct and sincere words spoken to everyone from the heart, always in freedom, gratuity, and truth.

We who are acutely aware of the treasury of grace received —thanks to the river of teaching and innumerable, vibrant catecheses flowing during all these years from Mother Elvira's heart and voice—offer you these pages at this time when her gaze is more alive, more transparent, and more luminous, even though her spoken word and her memory have become more fragile.

It is a time in which her eyes speak more than her mouth

. . .

a time in which, after the strong wind, the fire, and the
earthquake, we hear the tenderness of the light breeze . . .
a time more of embraces and smiles than of words . . .
a time in which her presence speaks more than words . . .
a time that is more of the heart than of the mind.

It is a time in which her amazement at revisiting and contemplating everything as "new" helps us to perceive that we are part of a story that is not ours, a story that amazes and marvels us more every day.

It is a time in which the echo of her teachings resounds powerfully in us, making us feel the great but serene responsibility of the treasure we received, a precious treasure — of that we are certain — that is not only for us. It is a treasure to give away!

Because of this, we welcomed the proposal of this book, certain that God's Providence asks this of us and wants it right now. We do not want to put Mother Elvira or the Community at the center of these pages. Telling you a little of her and our story, we simply desire to give glory to God the Father for the love He has poured out on us. We are a Community of the poor, of sinners, of fragile and wounded people, of people who were once dead and have risen to life again. We desire through these poor but truthful words to testify with infinite gratitude to the immense mercy of God for us. Pray for us. Thank You!

—Comunità Cenacolo
(Community of the Cenacle/Upper Room)

In life, the one who stands on his feet
is the one who learned how to stay on his knees.

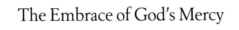

The Embrace of God's Mercy

Start to Count

Francesco, after having lived in our Community for a while, went home to "verify" how he would feel and act with his family. "La verifica" (a home visit for self-assessment after about two years in Community) is always an important time for the young men and women who come to Comunità Cenacolo asking for help to be "resurrected." They also need to be reborn in the relationships with their families, who frequently have left profound wounds in their hearts. "La verifica" serves toward this purpose.

For this reason, before he left Community to go home, I told Francesco what I always advise the young men and women who are especially wounded in their relationships with their fathers. "Go home," I tell them, "and when you see your father at a distance, run, run, run to meet him. Then wrap him in your arms and embrace him. Hug him tight and, while you embrace him, count up to seven without letting him go: one ... two ... three ... four ... five ... six ... seven. After a few seconds you'll see that he'll try to pull away from you, but you squeeze him even tighter and then he, too, will embrace you even tighter. Then after these seven seconds, let him go and look right into his eyes. Your father will cry. You'll cry. Everybody will cry. You will have made that man become a father again."

In those seven seconds, each person stops and remembers what he experienced in the past. Above all, what he failed to do in the past emerges. Both re-embrace their personal stories and personal roots. This gesture pierces the heart, coming from the deepest place within, and softens the hardest heart, yielding the fruit of peace that is born from forgiveness.

Like so many others, Francesco returned with radiant eyes and told me, "Elvira, when I saw my father approaching, I said to myself, 'Francesco, if you don't go now, you will never, ever go.' So I took a deep breath and started to run. I hugged him tight. I didn't let go when he tried to pull away. I counted to seven in my head, squeezing him tight ... and both us started to cry like babies, forgiving each other."

Francesco is one of so many young men and women who has experienced the power of the embrace of mercy. Many young adults, who have knocked on the door of the Community throughout the world, know well the power and freedom born in their hearts from this merciful embrace. I give them this advice because I experienced this myself. The encounter with God made me embrace my own poor life, my own wounded story, and freed me from the shame I felt about my father's fragility, giving me freedom, peace, and joy.

I also want to say this to each one of you: let yourselves be embraced by the tenderness of the mercy of God. Embrace your own life and your existence once again. God's presence is in your personal story. Seek Him, and you will find Him. You will encounter Him.

He was there in the darkest pages of our lives. He suffered with us. He was on the Cross with us and for us. Only He knows how to transform our darkness into light. Only He can transform our misery and poverty into a richness to be lived as a gift for our brothers and sisters. This is what I have experienced in my own personal life and what I contemplate today in the lives of all those we welcome in Community.

I am unceasingly aware of the fact that the story I have lived, and that I am still living, wasn't my own idea or my own plan. I am the first to be constantly surprised at what has happened, and what is still happening, in the life of Comunità Cenacolo, which is a work of God, the Holy Spirit, and Mary.

How could I have ever invented a story like this?

And I want to tell you the story ... with an embrace ... with the embrace of these pages. You start to count, too.

1

To Serve Is to Reign

My Childhood and My Vocation

Rather, God chose the foolish of the world
to shame the wise, and God chose the weak
of the world to shame the strong.

—1 Corinthians 1:27

It is always difficult to describe yourself. I am a passionate woman. I go from the broom to the stove, from the poor brother to the chapel. I am a woman in love with Life and in love with Love. I believe in the beauty, the truth, and the good that God has put in the heart of every man.

I am a simple woman, not sophisticated, who "walks" hours and hours on her knees, but who then runs with the poor, the blind, the deaf, the mute, and the lame. I'm a little like them, too.

I have never thought about learning to read or study in order to teach others how to "do" charity. Charity is my life. It is the gift of myself. It is the gift of my joy to give a more truthful and passionate "yes" to God. I am a woman who is astonished every day, who marvels contemplating God's works.

It is always a little embarrassing to talk about yourself, giving testimony and telling stories; however, I do it here voluntarily precisely out of gratitude to God! I have no human qualifications to speak or to teach. I am a daughter of poor parents, and I went only as far as third grade. At home I had to serve others. There was no time to study. The mercy of God reached down to me, and today I feel like a witness. Yes, I do! I speak because for years I have been a living witness of the Resurrection of Jesus that is renewed in the lives of the young people of the Community. When I encounter them, they are dead. Then, little by little, I contemplate them rising to new life. Today I have the courage to speak because it is time to evangelize, to give testimony.

First of all, a big "thank you" to God, who wanted my life. I believe that at the moment in which Papa and Mama conceived me, God's will already existed for something beautiful, great, and fruitful for others. I am happy to live, giving my life for others. I feel that it is enriching, especially for me. I am rich because, from the time I was a child, sacrifice taught me to give myself to others, to serve, to smile, and to overcome difficulty without a "long face," without saying, "I can't do it." I am happy to find myself still in the school of service. Everything that I learned in life, I learned serving.

I come from a large family. We lived during the period after the war of 1940-1945, with all the poverty and discomforts of the time. We were a poor immigrant family from Sora in central Italy, living in Alexandria to be near my father's work. Because we were a family from the south, they gave us a house that was barely the size of a chicken coop; nobody wanted people from the south because they had too many children. Everywhere we lived, I saw that there were other families, other children like me, who were living another reality, richer materially than mine.

I remember something my mother repeated to me every time she found me with friends who were better off than I was. When we had a piece of bread in our house— and during the war, it wasn't easy to have bread—or when we had cherries, Mama told me, "Remember, Rita, that all mouths are sisters! You can't put something in your mouth without giving something to someone else." Even in the hardship of poverty, she formed us in actions of solidarity that meant "family."

I am truly a daughter of the poor, but today I am deeply happy. Poverty is beautiful! We are more important than things, more important than riches, and more important than ambitions.

I am happy I was born at a time in history when not everyone had enough food to eat, and we got up from the table still
feeling hungry, because this taught us to sacrifice. I understood
that material and physical poverty could not destroy the unity
in charity of the family. I realized that true peace and well-being
are dimensions of the heart. We feel them when we are good and
generous. It is when we give to others that we become a universal
family who together and in truth can pray, "Our Father."

When I was still a child, I came to know God who is Father,
and immediately I learned to trust Him. I recall that when poverty
was most cruel, moments when the Cross was heaviest, I would
frequently hear my mother's lips repeat this prayer: "Holy Cross of
God, do not abandon us!" She said it in our dialect. This prayer
to God has always touched me so much.

I had a strong, demanding mother. Papa often lost his job
because of his weakness and wasn't always a help to the family.
In those moments, my mother didn't rebelliously say, "My God,
what have you done? How will we make it? Get him a job!"
Instead, in pain yet with faith, she would repeat, "Holy Cross of
God, do not abandon us!" She loved the Cross. She clung to it.
She found her strength in the Cross.

Nobody wants to suffer, but thanks to my mother's words, I
came to understand how important it is in life to embrace the
Cross. The Cross is our mother, and we must love her in order
to live well. We experienced this in our family.

When we had some money, my father would spend it drinking.
My father, Antonio, liked to drink too much wine. When I was a
child, this upset me and made me feel ashamed, especially when
he came drunk to pick me up at school in front of my classmates
who made fun of me. I recall how he would come to meet me
with his bicycle, staggering, and the children would mock me,

saying, "Look, Rita, your father is drunk again!" I felt humiliated, because I understood that alcoholism wasn't something good. However, those situations taught me what sacrifice means, what humility means. Reflecting now, I understand that my father, in spite of his fragility, at least came to get me at school. Back then, many fathers didn't go to pick up their children, and today they never go.

My father didn't hesitate to wake me up in the middle of the night and tell me, "Rita, go buy me cigarettes!" I remember very well.... I had to walk a long way on a dark street. I tried to run fast, singing to conquer my fear. At night the sprawling tree branches seemed like long, threatening arms. When I arrived at the tobacconist, I would knock, and the shopkeeper would get up grumbling and give me some cigarettes. I would dash home to make my father happy.

When I encountered God, all this suffering in our family was transformed and enlightened. Today I can say that my father was for me the university that taught me how to love and to serve everyone with dignity. He was the first poor, broken person that I had to welcome, love, and serve.

I relate these things in order to give glory to God for giving me a father who was not afraid to be who he was. I don't want to justify my father's mistakes, but we need to remember that no one is born a parent. We learn little by little. Most assuredly the Holy Spirit was using him, thinking of the mission God had prepared for me. My father's fragility was my first school of life. It formed and shaped me.

Today, in light of my story, I teach the young men and women to love, respect, and forgive their fathers and mothers, as I have done. This is possible only if they encounter their heavenly Father, who comes first before their earthly fathers and mothers.

A father like mine must have suffered deeply in his child-hood. We must show so much mercy toward others, as others have shown us. I loved my father. I served him faithfully. For this reason, I am not ashamed to talk about him. When you love, you are not ashamed.

Today, and each day more and more, I am happy to be alive, to have been born, and even happier because the Lord has always put me in a position not to be able to worry about myself. I've never had much time in my life to think about myself, how I was feeling, if I was happy or sad, good or bad. I always had to take care of others and serve them. I'm convinced that there is no kingdom more fascinating, greater, more amazing, or richer than the heart of man. To serve is truly to experience the privilege of reigning!

I often think, "How good the Lord has been to me!" He has loved, followed, and molded me since I was a child. When I was seventeen years old, I was in a serious relationship with a young man, who loved me very much. In my time, we spoke of love — we did not "make" love. We had already decided to have many children ... and then something happened inside me. At a certain moment I began to ask myself, "All my life with him? Only with him? Only for him? No, I couldn't ever. This is not my path." It felt too limiting to me. There was another spouse knocking at the door of my heart, who opened it wide. It was Jesus, Son of the carpenter of Nazareth, who by profession was also a carpenter. It was He who would me a make me a happy spouse.

At nineteen, I left my family. It caused so much suffering, especially for my mother, who had to work to sustain the fam-ily. She counted on me to take care of my siblings, so I was the anchor for the home. None of my brothers or sisters supported my decision. My decision to become a nun made no sense to them.

In spite of all this, the call was strong. It was stronger than human affections, stronger than blood, stronger than the flesh, stronger than the problems at home, stronger than the objections of others, stronger than my own understanding.

It was March 8, 1956, the day young women entered the convent. I got up early in the morning and, with a small cardboard box, I departed in silence. At the station, while I was getting on the train, I heard the unmistakable sound of my mother's wooden clogs. Wrapped in a shawl, she had been following me. She understood that there was something moving inside me, that I was preparing myself for a journey, and that I was leaving for good. Our eyes met. In her eyes there were so many questions: "Rita, what are you doing? Are you leaving us? Are you really going? How will we make it?" I looked at her ... and I got on the train.

Later I always blamed myself for that moment, because it seemed to me that I had not understood my mother's pain, until one day a young man, listening to this story, said to me: "Elvira, thank God you got on that train. Otherwise, all of us would still be desperate and waiting! All of us were on that train with you!"

It's true! Today I realize that so many others were leaving with me on that train. I thank God that He didn't let me turn back. If I had done so, I would be much poorer. I wouldn't have seen all the beautiful things that God has worked through my poor story. That trip continues, and today I am much richer in life, in goodness, in light, in peace, and in joy.

I arrived at a convent of the Sisters of Charity in Borgaro, Turin, which is still flourishing today. This convent was founded by St. Giovanna Antida, a great French foundress, who gave her life in service of the poor, excluding no one. I, Rita Agnese Petrozzi, became Sister Elvira in this community, where I remained for about twenty-eight years. I served in different ways, but especially as the cook for many years. Serving others was always a great joy for me.

Later on, within me, a fire was lit. A strong desire grew within me to commit myself to young people, especially those who were searching for meaning in their lives. I saw them wandering aimlessly on the streets and in the public squares. It seemed to me that they were crying out their need for life and for truth. They screamed out by taking drugs, numbing themselves, despairing, and letting themselves die day by day. They wanted to know if love exists, if there is truly hope, if it is possible to have interior peace, if their story could be reborn. I read this in their eyes and in their bad choices.

I saw them like "sheep without a shepherd," without direction, although financially secure with money in their pockets, a car, an education, and everything they could want materially, yet their hearts filled with sadness and death.

In prayer, kneeling before the Eucharist, I intensely felt that I could perceive—almost physically—their cry of pain, their need for help. I felt within me a push that wasn't my own, that I could not suppress, that grew more and more. It wasn't an idea. Even I didn't know what was happening, but I felt that I must give those young people something that God had placed inside me for them.

I asked my superiors again and again to allow me to do something for them, but rightly so, they said that I would be venturing into the unknown, that I was unprepared, that I hadn't studied and didn't know anything about the problems of youth, so I really wouldn't be able to make it. All these valid reasons made me wait, suffer, and pray. The fire never went out.

For me, it was like living in agony, waiting to see how the Holy Spirit would develop what was churning inside me. I suffered so much because it seemed as if I was wasting time. In reality, it was God's time, and I had to wait for His moment, the hour in which I could finally dedicate myself to the young people in order to protect them, form them, and love them. I had so many tempting thoughts: "Why don't they trust me?" But then I said to myself, "Why should they trust me? I'm just a poor creature who wants to 'fly.'"

Some people said, "Elvira, why don't you leave your religious order? That way you can do what you want!" But I didn't intend to "do what I wanted." What was happening to me was very different from that. I wanted to have the certainty that what I had within me wasn't something of mine, but of God. I was certain this would come through obedience. With so much trust and hope, I waited ... praying, suffering, loving, and continuing to ask for many years until one day my superiors trusted me and said, "Okay!"

Now, at seventy years of age, I reason a little more, and I understand that all this was a blessing. These were the labor pains. Today I am very close to those who were my superiors. We are friends, and many of the sisters are as amazed as I am at what happened. They know me, so they really understand that this comes from God, certainly not from me.

For many years now, the sisters of St. Giovanna Antida Thouret have had a Cenacolo house for twenty young men in Borgaro, Turin, where I was welcomed as a novice. Our presence there has always been a great joy and blessing for me, a sign of our close friendship in the Lord and in the service of the poor, a bond stronger than the difficulties we had on the journey.

In fact, in the next few years, as Cenacolo grew, we needed to take further steps for the new work of God and its unexpected expansion. With great suffering for me and for them, I had to leave my religious order. Today I still ask myself the reason for this sacrifice, this "cut" that made me bleed, but throughout these years, the words of so many friends comforted me: "Elvira, God wanted something new to be born!"

Today I remember the past as a blessing. Recalling my childhood and everything I experienced, I can say that it was a beautiful story, precisely because it was mingled with so many shadows. God's grace was abundant in the midst of so much human poverty.

It's evident that, in the midst of all the chaos of the war and the uncertainty we experienced in the family, the Holy Spirit was forming me in charity, compassion, and service, preparing me to help those who were suffering more than I was. First my parents and then my superiors were already, in a certain sense, inspired and guided by the hand of the Holy Spirit, who was preparing me for what I am living today.

God does great things with people who know they are small. The smaller and poorer we feel, the more the Lord will do great things through the Community. (from the *Rule of Life* of Comunità Cenacolo)

2

The First Steps

The First House

The stone the builders rejected
has become the cornerstone.

—Psalm 118:22

After years of waiting and prayer, the superiors permitted me to leave. At that moment, after the labor pains, Comunità Cenacolo was finally born. This plan of tenderness and mercy that God the Father had for the young people became a reality.

We began in a house on a hill, loaned to us without cost by the town of Saluzzo. As Sisters of Charity, we developed our apostolate at the kindergarten Regina Margherita, so I was already familiar with the people in the area. I knew that on that hill there was an abandoned house, owned by the town, which was available for charitable activities. I asked the authorities for permission to use it in order to welcome young and needy persons, and with courage and openness, the town granted it. Thus, on July 16, the feast of Our Lady of Mount Carmel, I was given the keys to begin the work.

When I saw that gate open, I simply gave a great sigh of relief. I was overjoyed! Life exploded inside me! It was the joy that had been won by the long time of waiting. Finally, my desires were being fulfilled.

Among the bramble and rubble, my gaze caught a glimpse of a small statue of Our Lady over the portal of the main entrance. Seeing that Mary was already there, waiting for us and welcoming us, confirmed the desires in our hearts and made me exult with joy even more.

When we arrived, we found exactly what you would find when a house has been abandoned: brush and debris, broken doors, windows without glass. The people who had accompanied me were wringing their hands when they saw this desolate, abandoned place as if to say, "How can anyone live here?" But I saw it already rebuilt and renovated, full of young people of joy and of true freedom, exactly as it is today.

Joining me were Nives, a teacher whom I had known during my time in Saluzzo, and Sister Aurelia, a sister from my religious order who asked to follow me. We began with the ardor, the strength, and the beauty of love. We did everything with so much enthusiasm and joy: the cleanup and the renovation. We worked day and night, but I never feared the sacrifices nor thought of what we did as a hardship.

It's true. We had nothing. We slept on the ground; our first benches and tables were the broken shutters from the house. There was nothing . . . there was everything! When there is nothing, there is always so much more: more solidarity, more love, more smiles, and sometimes more tears, but it doesn't matter. Life is like this. It is made of light and shadow, courage and fear, strength and weakness. The love among us was alive. It was stronger than the adversity, fear, or failure.

Many asked me what I wished to accomplish, what idea I had in my head. They said to me, "Elvira, make a plan! Explain what you wish to do, where you want to go, and what you need." I had no idea what a plan even looked like! I didn't have any plan of my own. At that time there were so many things to do that I wasn't thinking of anything. I didn't have time. I never remember ever planning anything, not in my head, much less on paper. I was never in a hurry. I was convinced in my heart that the One who called me to do this would indicate the path to take a day at a time.

It could have all been a failure, but in that moment, I never thought that it could be a failure, because inside me there was a strength of love that wasn't a human love or only my love. I didn't know if I was capable of loving, but inside me there was this courage that was not mine alone, a capacity to risk, to see beyond the present, to believe against every failure. Now I can say that it was the love of God that invaded my will, my freedom, my strength, and my weakness. In that moment, I rediscovered my faith. I found a concrete faith, an incarnate faith, a faith of works, a faith that takes risks.

The hour of God had finally arrived. The gate was opened, and I was dancing with joy. One step after another, we discovered God's will for us with amazement.

The name "Cenacolo" (Cenacle, or Upper Room) was not my idea. There was a priest who came to live for a short time with the young men. He suggested this name, and I accepted it, because I welcomed the advice that was given to me — and then I did what the *Lord* wanted! I wanted Mary there at all costs. Thinking about the Upper Room, I immediately thought of the Church, of the Apostles gathered with Mary in the Cenacle, behind a locked door and full of fear after Jesus' death. However, they were praying with Mary in the Cenacle. The Holy Spirit descended, and the Apostles were transformed into courageous witnesses. That door, closed out of fear, burst wide open through the courage and joy of their testimony.

Today I believe this name was a prophecy. It was the name that best represented what we wanted to be. Even the young people who come to us are full of fear, very closed and withdrawn, mute in thought and word, with much sadness, loneliness, and restlessness in their hearts. Mary gathers them together and brings them here, where we pray with her. The Holy Spirit descends upon them and little by little makes them new young men and women, free and courageous testimonies of the resurrection.

With the passing of the years, the motherhouse was renovated, thanks to the work of the young men and the help of so many friends. Today it shines in all its beauty. So many other houses have been born, but the adventure of renovation is not yet finished. The Community is a lifelong workshop that is always open. Each day, every day, is a wonder and a marvel. Now the marvel and the beauty are in the smiles of the young people, in their luminous eyes, in the joy that is reflected in their faces and in the tenacity and strength that they demonstrate by choosing to be in a Community that describes itself as "demanding." Yes, demanding!

We want to love — not pretending to believe, but truly believing that young people, even when they have failed, still have a potential that hasn't been ignited. We welcome them as they are. We welcome them in order to love them in their need today without thinking of tomorrow. At the same time, however, we want them to understand that *they can do it* and have a future, for when things are done with love, passion, and will, life can be rebuilt. We expect all this from them precisely because we love them. It is a love that aims to restore their dignity. They are not old, sick, or physically handicapped. They are young men and women who have lost their way, and they have the right to find it again, to rediscover that their lives have value, that within them is a treasure of goodness, will, strength, and love that they must discover and believe in.

We started out in a demolished, abandoned house, just like the lives of the young people who knocked on our doors. As they rebuilt the walls, the young men rebuilt their willpower, their trust in themselves, and their futures. I told them, "Here no one pays your way! You must earn your lives through your own sweat, step after step, rock after rock, discovering that within you is the strength and dignity of a new life." And they believed.

We were born in an abandoned house without any financial security. Everything is the work of God and the struggles of many brothers and sisters. We often think of our roots, poor but beautiful, rich in faith, sacrifice, joy, and living prayer. (from the *Rule of Life* of Comunità Cenacolo)

3

Finally, You Have Arrived

Welcoming

As the sparrow finds a home
and the swallow a nest to settle her young,
my home is by your altars,
Lord of hosts, my king and my God!

—Psalm 84:4

At the beginning of our time in Saluzzo, I saw a man arrive at the gate, and I went to meet him. He had a sad look, full of shame and disappointment with life. His face betrayed the anger he felt toward himself, life, everyone. I felt in my heart that I had to say these simple words, so, while looking into his eyes and holding his hand, I said: "I was waiting for you. Finally, you have arrived!" Looking up, his eyes filled with tears, and his heart melted. Trust was reborn in him. Sometime later, he related that he had never known his father or his mother. He was abandoned at birth, and no one in his life had ever waited for him or loved him. He grew up in orphanages, filled with anger toward everyone. That day, for the first time in his life, he felt loved like a son finally welcomed by his mother. That man is still with us today, because where love is found, life is good.

From that moment, those words, "Finally you have arrived," have been repeated through words or gestures for each young person who knocks at our door. To feel loved, one must feel that someone has been waiting for him.

At the beginning, my collaborators and I planned to spend a month together in order to bond, pray more, and live together in preparation for this new life. A few days later, however, three guys came to the gate and, looking right in our eyes, asked: "Is this the community for drug addicts?"

We hadn't defined our work as a "community for drug addicts," but a community of young people, lost in meaninglessness, boredom, and insecurities, incapable of starting or finishing anything. And there were so many of them! In fact, often their mothers would lament about these sons and daughters. We came to know them through their mothers' trust, as they shared their pain with us. We looked at one another and said, "Drug addict or not, they are young people," so we said, "Yes!"

And so it began with these three who entered our community and adapted to the poverty of the moment. In the first days, not having furnishings, they slept on the grass that was cut during the day. It was July and not a discomfort to curl up on the grass or to sleep on the pavement. They accepted the privations of the moment with simplicity because we lived it together; it was like this for everyone. They were, in a way, our first Providence, because they began by helping us, putting rooms in order and cleaning all around.

And thus, our story began. Honestly, in my heart I thought, "We will welcome about fifty young men in this house, and after that we will begin the therapy." I didn't know whether to call this proposal "therapy," because deep down I did not see them as sick. They didn't have ulcers or cancer. They were young people with death in their eyes, already dead in their hearts. They didn't ask me for medicine, but for the will to live.

What was the therapy? What did I have to propose to them that is true, authentic, and enduring? Due to the honesty I felt in my heart toward them, I didn't want to betray, deceive, or disappoint them in any way. I was aware that human therapy alone would not satisfy their hearts or give their troubled consciences the peace of forgiveness. I reflected on the times in life when my own heart was wounded, my eyes were spent, and I felt disappointment in my heart.

I recalled that prayer rekindled my hope, raised my head, and let me believe again that tomorrow I could do it. They themselves confirmed that this was the right path, by asking me to teach them a life of prayer as we journeyed together on this path that had helped me, as well as so many others. Now it would help them, too.

We began this journey that didn't end with just fifty guys, as I first thought. They continued to arrive at the gate, and they did not come asking for money or food; instead, they said, "I want to live. I'm tired. I want to live. I'm dying. I want to live!" They were asking us for life!

With their eyes, their tears, their pain, and destroyed physically, they asked us for life. Those already in Community would say to me, "Elvira, welcome him. I'll give him my bed. I'll sleep on the floor tonight. Let's welcome him. He needs it." Seeing their compassion and desire to help one another gave me courage and trust. So we went forward.

I have to admit that we made some mistakes in the beginning. For example, we thought we were doing something good by giving the guys ten cigarettes a day. We did this for a couple of years, knowing that other communities did the same, but I confess that it really bothered me to see a guy distribute these cigarettes every day after lunch. Finally, I understood that I had to exercise the authority the Lord had given me for these young people, with truth and strength without exception.

I strongly perceived it at a particular moment in 1986 when I went to Medjugorje for the first time. During the pilgrimage the thought struck me and my heart confirmed this truth: "I am not faithful to these young people." I asked myself if cigarettes, fundamentally, were a drug for those who came here precisely to free themselves from every type of drug. I knew that I had to be stronger and more demanding.

As a result, one evening after I returned, I knelt before them in the chapel at Saluzzo and said, "Guys, I ask for your forgiveness. I have betrayed you, because I did not have faith in you. You came here to be helped to live in true freedom from all addiction, but I let you keep cigarettes because I was afraid that you would suffer and leave. From now on, there is no more smoking in Comunità Cenacolo! You are all free to leave, but know that if you would like to come back, the Community will welcome you immediately."

I turned to the most problematic guy regarding cigarettes, who by now was a man, and I said to him: "Domenico, go get a bag. All of you who still have cigarettes in your pockets must place them in the bag if you want to remain in the Community."

As Domenico passed the young men, they reached their hands in their pockets and, with difficulty and suffering, looked at one another and threw away their last cigarettes, which would have lasted until lunch the next day. Much to my surprise, they all threw them away.

Then, while they made a bonfire in the yard, I went into the office and took all the cigarettes that we had, brought them out, and burned them. All of them stood around watching. At a certain point, several of them got guitars and began to sing, while others danced around the fire. Some cried, while others tried to take their last drag of smoke.

It was a joy to see them so generous, courageous, and willing. They were telling me that they preferred life, that life is worth more, so much more, than cigarettes. Not one of them left. I said to them very sincerely, "I am waiting. If anyone wants to go, I'll get the money for the train." But no one left. All of them stayed.

After about fifteen days, however, one of the boys, Walter, told me: "Elvira, it's too difficult for me to be without cigarettes.

I can't make it," and he left. Then six months later he returned. We welcomed him back, and he began again.

It often happens like this. We have never judged a young man whose attitude differed from ours. In these situations we have always said: "We must be courageous enough to trust and go forward! He has seen the light. He'll come back!"

In the beginning, some would say, "They are men. They need to drink at least one glass of wine," so we gave it to them, but this created disagreements and conflict. We looked at one another in dismay. Sometimes the guys would ask us if they could go out in public a bit.

We thought, "After all, they are men. They're adults. They know what they're doing. One has been here for three months, another for two, another for one, and the other for six months." We gave them some money and told them, "Go out, grab a coffee, and then come back." We thought that it was right to keep them in touch with society, not completely exclude them from the world.

It went well the first time and the second. Then one evening they returned drunk out of their minds, punching one another. Everybody wanted to leave. We were afraid for a moment, but I raised my voice with strength and clarity that I knew wasn't mine. They looked at me, stunned, and listened. They calmed down, a little scared. Then they went to bed in silence. We waited for their drunkenness to pass, and the next day it was all over. They told me, "Elvira, we can't handle freedom or overcome temptation. We don't need an escape or appeasements. This is the life we need!" I understood they wanted a demanding love from me. I shouldn't think of them as "poor things," cut off from the world, needing money to walk around the city in order to be happy. This isn't what they wanted.

It wasn't easy at the beginning. We had to learn everything. We had our dramatic moments, and, at times, we saw the hell they had in their hearts, the strength of evil that was crushing them. We witnessed it all! However, this made us stronger in our prayer, more convinced of God's love. They needed the love of God, not only our compassion, rules, and limits. They needed God!

We intensified our prayer, getting on our knees before the Eucharist. We were the first to believe and be convinced that the solution was prayer, a relationship with God, returning to the Father like the prodigal son who once again feels embraced, forgiven, and healed in his heart.

Everything we experienced with them has been our "school of life," our university, that teaches us what evil can do in a young person's heart. I am not afraid to say that my teachers, experts, and books have been the guys themselves. I've turned the pages and learned to read the book of life with them in these years. It holds within it the mystery of the Cross, pages written with pain, wounds, and anger, but I've also contemplated pages of mercy, forgiveness, goodness, joy, simplicity, and resurrection.

My human, Christian, and religious advancement came from the young men. They taught me everything. I wanted to be the first to learn from them, to be a student of their school. Who could teach me how to help them find freedom from the drama in their hearts, if not they themselves?

From the very beginning, the guys taught me the importance of accepting their families, involving them on the path of their rebirth. I asked parents, and I continue to ask them, for so much … their conversion! Almost always parents prefer to pay a fee, especially when they are desperate. When parents bring me their son, they put their hands in their wallets and ask, "Sister, what must I pay so that my son can stay here? What does it cost?" I always say that their sons' lives are not paid for with money. They already had too much money, and they are ruined by it! I say to each father and mother, "We don't want money. We want a collaboration that involves your life, your choices, and your daily activities. You must walk together with him. The rebirth of your son is paid for with your conversion."

I ask parents to pray that God's truth may enter into the family and illuminate what they have done wrong, because the failure of the drug-addict son is also, to a degree, their failure as a couple. The parents feel at fault, and they blame themselves. The sense of fault that is often dumped on a spouse must become truth in each one's conscience, truth and forgiveness. I tell the parents, "The greatest source of power for the salvation of your son is your own conversion, that you be united to save him. When parents convert, their child is saved!"

Many parents who live the experience of a lost son or daughter as a cross they are not able to resolve, delegate the solution of the problem to someone else; but that cross, which brings them to their knees, becomes the source of their conversion. What seemed to be a disgrace for the entire family, God transformed into conversion for everyone and a rediscovery of the true values in life. Truly our God, only He, can transform the darkness into light and draw forth good where evil seemed to triumph.

Often the young men are living hatred, anger, rejection, and judgment toward their parents. They bear the weight of deep wounds that have lacerated their souls since childhood, unhealed wounds that then became open doors to the action of evil. Slowly, with prayer, the discovery of forgiveness, and seeing their parents live differently, they transform that hatred into understanding. The reciprocal accusations are transformed into truth with oneself, and each learns to forgive and be forgiven.

After some time spent on this journey, the young people recognize that they have been too violent, pretentious, and demanding toward their parents. When they see their parents again, they ask for forgiveness. As parents embrace their children and sons and daughters embrace their parents, we have seen an abundance of tears, tears of reconciliation and tears of resurrected families.

I chose to believe in young people, and I still believe in them. It's not true that they are lazy, fearful, and indifferent. It's not true! They are capable of struggling, sharing, and making sacrifices. Right from the beginning, they grasped that drugs weren't our main focus, but rather rebuilding their lives together with our own through a journey of truth. And they responded!

We trusted, for faith taught us not to fear; faith nurtured our hope, trust, and patience, placing our security in the God that I knew in my heart. He gave me more of a guarantee than any human security!

> We are called, as Community, to share our lives, to serve. Only if you believe that "nothing is impossible for God" will you be able to believe that even the man in whom no one hopes can rise to new life and smile and love life once again. (from the *Rule of Life* of Comunità Cenacolo)

4

The Door of the Heart

Spirituality

He was praying in a certain place, and when he
had finished, one of his disciples said to him, "Lord,
teach us to pray just as John taught his disciples." He
said to them, "When you pray, say: Father ..."

—Luke 11:1-2

When we opened the doors of the house, there was not yet a chapel. In the morning, while the young men were waking up and going into the fields to work, we prayed the Rosary and the Psalms in a little room. In the beginning, we did not have a plan of prayer for the young men because we thought, "We will accept man as he is. Man is made in the image of God; therefore, he already is a prayer for us who have faith."

After a little more than a month, there was a great surprise. One of the guys, instead of going to work, woke up early and came to the small, poor chapel and sat next to me. He asked me, "What are you doing?" I said, "We're praying." He said, "May I pray too?" and he stayed.

We were praying a psalm, and he also read a verse. Then, in the days that followed, another young man came to pray, then another and another. After a week, they were all there to pray with us.

I realized they weren't asking for a roof over their heads, a plate of food, a bed, but to find God. They were hungry and thirsty for Him. As they woke up early to pray in the chapel with us, I perceived this request and need: "Teach us to pray. We want to know the Lord. We need Him!" This is how the proposal of prayer and faith became the foundation of this journey of rebirth.

Obviously, when many of the young men enter the Community, they say, "I don't believe in Jesus. I don't care about God. I don't want to pray!" I respond, "Don't worry about it. We are not interested in whether or not you believe in God. He believes in you, and we believe *for* you. You came here to be freed not only from drugs but also from your fears and from your entire past. You just try to trust, and you'll see. Start your journey. We believe in you."

Others, with an attitude of mistrust, but above all with a mixture of sadness and longing on their faces, are almost conscious of their need to see, to touch, and to feel God to be able to live again. They tell me, "But I don't see or hear the living God, the risen One that you talk about!" I answer, "But you, have you opened the door to Him? Have you ever tried telling Him for even a second, 'Lord, I need you. Help me!' The door of the heart has only one handle, the one on the inside. Only we, in our freedom, can open it to the One who knocks, to Him who desires to enter to make us happy, so that our joy may be full. Ask Him for help. Open the door of your heart. Let Him come … and you will be happy!"

Still others shake their heads: "Sister, I don't understand!" Then I respond, "We welcome you freely when no one else wants you. We don't ask you for anything but trust. You can't understand with your head why you should pray before a simple piece of bread. We don't expect you to understand with your reason. We simply say to you that, if you want, you can experience what has happened in us. If you try, a miracle will happen within you. Your heart will change. You'll see!"

Then, when I see them again after a few months, I notice that their eyes are more alive, and there are smiles on their faces. I ask them, "Do you feel like you did when you arrived?" They say, "No, I feel changed." I see a new light in their eyes.

Through the years, some people have mocked me, saying that I want to save all desperate youth with a bunch of Hail Marys and that it doesn't make sense to propose prayer. Above all, they say that it is not right.

I accepted what they said, but I never took it to heart. I even smiled, but I always went forward, following what I felt to be the truth. When they would tell me, "Man and his freedom come first, then God," I listened and thought, "But who would man be without God?" In fact, the young men themselves told me they want to encounter and know Him.

We propose prayer because I want them to experience faith, not as something theoretical, but as an encounter that changes you and transforms your life, giving you peace with yourself and with others. Ultimately, the guys are free to decide. I am aware that not all of them will choose the Christian life immediately or fully; but if no one proposes this path, if nobody helps you live it or points it out to you, how could you ever come to know it?

I receive letters daily from those who, years after leaving us, confess that for a little while they lost the faith. They forgot all about it. They slipped, but then they found God again. They felt the nostalgia of all the good they had lived and felt the need to pray and believe in Him. I am certain that if you encounter the goodness of the Lord, if someone has loved you in the name of the Lord and shown you the true face of God, this leaves an indelible mark. Sooner or later in life, you'll return to Him, for nowhere else can you find the peace and joy your heart experienced living in His presence.

I am certain that, in proposing God and helping others to have an encounter with His Mercy, I am serving man and desiring his true good. This is an act of honesty.

The experience of prayer is lived by the youth in a simple yet concrete way. The guys often tell me, "When I pray, I feel better." So it is! When you pray, you don't realize it, but you change. If you are a guy who is angry, you become calmer. I say, "guy," but I can also say it about myself. The more I pray, the more patient and compassionate I am. God's mercy is within me more. Whoever prays well, lives well!

Prayer is the nourishment that transforms life and is the answer to the deep interior desires you've carried for so long. For many years now, I've contemplated this miracle of prayer, which is real, actual, and true.

Mary and the Eucharist are our two treasures. From the beginning, the Rosary has highlighted the day in the Community. On this holy crown hang the resurrected lives of so many youth who have passed through Cenacolo, as well as many desperate families who have rediscovered peace, serenity, and forgiveness in this simple but powerful school of prayer.

In the Community, we pray one Rosary early in the morning, one in the afternoon, and another one in the evening. Why? Precisely because it gives cadence to the dawn, the afternoon, and the sunset of life—to every aspect of our life. The dawn of each day is the beginning of our personal story, a new beginning to each day. For this reason, we fix our gaze on the birth of Jesus, and we meet Him due to Mary's "yes," so that our life, too, may be reborn, may begin again each day with Him, and may say "yes" to His plan of love for us.

Then there is the early afternoon, the time of adolescence that is often the most problematic age, where we search for deeper answers to our questions. When you are twelve, thirteen, fourteen years old, you begin to see your parents' flaws and you judge them. School begins to feel restrictive to you. The differences between rich and poor make you suffer. You do not know whose side to take. You struggle incredibly with your feelings, and sometimes you have an enormous conflict within yourself and with everything that surrounds you. It is a stage for which we educators are never fully prepared to give true, convincing answers to the profound questions that young people communicate to us through their protests.

That is why in the early afternoon, which represents that time of adolescence when so few answers were given to us, we pray the Sorrowful Mysteries, so that Jesus' Passion may heal our wounds, our negative memories, and the violent and angry judgments that, at that age, provoked false rebellion inside us and led us on the path of evil.

Then evening comes. Praying the Glorious Mysteries is our preparation for the years of weariness, the years of old age, sickness, and the sunset of life. Contemplating Christ's Resurrection, you prepare your heart for the definitive encounter with Him, and you discover that your suffering gives birth to a new life, which is the true reality that awaits you in heaven. With your rosary in your hands, you will not get discouraged, because you will have an extraordinary fullness, clarity of mind, and freedom of heart.

I am preparing myself for these years, and I truly desire to get there with light in my mind, joy in my heart, a living hope, and a courage that is present in every moment. Let us embrace, then, the entire day of life with this sweetest of prayers that, through Mary's heart, places our life story in Christ's life and His in our daily living. The Rosary is a prayer for the humble, for the poor, and for the simple. For this reason, it is Mary's prayer. She, simple and humble, has a heart as large as humanity, yet strong and powerful in God's eyes. When we pray to our Blessed Mother, we turn to her maternal, human heart that beats for the entire world.

We repeat Elizabeth's words with faith, when we say, "Blessed are you among women and blessed is the fruit of your womb,

Jesus." We see Our Lady pregnant. We receive from her arms that "Blessed Fruit" that she gives today to free us from our fears and from everything that we don't like about ourselves, the Fruit that nourishes and saves us.

The other treasure of our prayer, the true nourishment of the soul, is the Eucharist, much more satisfying than food for the body. Jesus has left us the world's most precious treasure, the most effective medicine for healing the wounds of the heart, the extraordinary light that leads us out of the darkness of evil.

I have proposed it to the young people because I have felt transformed before the living presence of Jesus, who remains among us. I can say that I am a living witness of what God works through the Eucharist. Often I compare our Community to a Eucharistic miracle.

In my life, the call to dedicate myself to the youth happened before the Eucharist when I was already a sister. There on my knees, I began to perceive the deep pain of so many young people on the streets and to hear their deep cry of solitude in my heart. The Eucharist makes you enter into the heart of the story that is inside you and those around you. I renewed my "yes" to Him, surrendering myself to this leap of faith that was inviting me to a new beginning. I felt Jesus sending me to go to those young people who walk in tatters in our town squares, with hearts saddened by drugs, hungering and thirsting for meaning in their lives that they have yet to find.

What therapeutic method or medicine could I offer them? No pill can give the joy of life or peace in the heart! Because of the love and respect I have for them, I did not want to deceive them in any way, so I offered them what comforted and helped me many times, reviving my trust and hope: the power of God's mercy and of Eucharistic prayer.

I pointed out the path that saved me many times, giving me dignity, strength, courage, constancy, peace, joy, and enthusiasm in my heart: kneeling with trust before Jesus in the Eucharist, so that He can raise us up again and make us go forward. When they are before the Lord, the "daily resurrection" happens in the hearts of our guys.

Being in adoration before that silent Presence reawakens their consciences and makes them cry out. It illuminates and sheds light on what is good and what is bad, bringing them back to God's mercy through the sacrament of forgiveness. This leads them to nourish themselves with the Body of Christ, which gives us strength for the journey. The truth of Christ becomes true, full freedom within us, the freedom that the young people we welcome were seeking here and on the streets of the world.

It's striking that the development of our Community is bound to the Eucharist, and that it creates not only a personal, but a communal dynamism. Initially, a few of our youth spontaneously got up in the middle of the night for Eucharistic adoration. Then, each Saturday night, which for them was the night of highs and darkness, they decided to kneel in adoration from 2:00 until 3:00 a.m. in all of our Community houses to pray for those who sought joy in the false illusions of the world.

Then another beautiful intuition was born, and someone said, "Elvira has gone crazy." For years, on the first Saturday of each month, we have opened our doors to all the youth who want to experience an evening of true joy together—an alternative to the discotheque—from which they can bring home hope, a smile, love, friendship, a feeling of unity, and belief in one another. This moment of strong faith and joy begins at 9:00 p.m. and ends at 1:30 a.m. At 2:00 a.m., we send all of them home!

What happens? What happens is what our Community is. Our Community opens the door to lots of young people and becomes a festival of music, dancing, joy, testimonies, and smiles—so much freedom, and so much love. Then, at a certain moment, amid the stupor and silence of all, the Guest of Honor arrives, the most important Friend! The sweet singing and the smiles continue while one of our priests enters with the monstrance, the presence of the Eucharistic Jesus. It is exposed on the altar and, with spontaneous prayers, everyone begins to thank and bless the Lord. Then, we adore Him in moments of profound silence, as we grasp our need for interior healing.

We want to tell to the young people, "You can't revisit certain past experiences without Jesus. Let Him look at you." We offer them these moments of silent introspection and interior truth in the presence of Jesus, not alone. In His presence, with hope in their hearts and the joy they experienced, they rediscover their faith. There are always priests available for confession to welcome their profound need to feel forgiven and sustained by God's mercy. At midnight sharp, in the middle of the night, we celebrate the joyful and luminous Sunday Eucharist.

Numerous young people attend. Many come out of curiosity, and others come faithfully. Some come with piercings and long hair. We decided to take the risk, saying, "We succeeded in our mission, even if only one of them realizes that it is possible to dance, play music, sing, rejoice, and experience a Saturday night, returning home with joy and something beautiful in his heart ... the peace of God."

The moment arrived on our Community journey when the young men decided to begin perpetual Eucharistic adoration. They gave me this as a gift many years ago on my birthday. The various houses decided to stay one hour a day in front of the

Lord in their respective chapels in order to cover every hour of the day.

This ushered the Community story into high gear. Young people arrived from everywhere, and the houses multiplied. The missions opened in Latin America for the children living on the streets. Community families chose to live in the mission, and the religious vocations of consecrated brothers and sisters were born.

The Eucharist is peace, encounter, amazement, strength, and risk. It gives you everything you need to live each day in the school of Jesus. You learn many things; above all, you learn love. In all these years, for me, a consecrated religious sister, the young people have been living testimony that the Eucharist is the living, true presence of the Risen One. Not only is the death and Resurrection of Jesus made present in the Eucharist, but our dead life, entering His, rises. I can truthfully testify that if one is in Christ, he is truly a new creation!

However, I proposed prayer composed not only of words but also of actions. Prayer isn't something you just say and do in the chapel. True prayer is lived beyond the chapel, at work. Prayer and work, *ora et labora*, are the pillars of our Community life.

Many of the young people worked before entering our Community. Some earned a lot of money while others traveled, but all of this was not enough to satisfy their hearts. Others never held a job, living in laziness on the streets. Their work was stealing, vandalizing, deceiving, and surviving one day at a time.

The reality of work, which occupies a good part of the day in the Community, is fundamental for rebuilding the interior life. The first job the young people must learn is to live.

As they work, they rebuild their willpower and they learn responsibility. They regain trust in themselves and see that they are capable of sacrifice, commitment, and consistency. They discover that they are enriched, not so much by what they do but by how they do it.

They experience that a dinner cooked with love is more nourishing and gives joy to the heart, that a job well done impacts the doer and causes those who see it to reflect, a room cleaned well gives peace and serenity to the soul.

Work in the Community is not an end in itself. It is not for nourishing pride or ambition or for earning money. It is not a false anchor of salvation or a place to escape during difficulties. Instead, it is an instrument of rebirth, building dialogue, growing in humility, discovering and using one's gifts to taste the joy of building something beautiful by sacrificing oneself. Work is the concrete measure of the truth of prayer, which manifests itself through service. He who prays well, works well. It is even more beautiful to carry it out together with others because a struggle unites those who share it. A sacrifice done together creates more friendship and happiness. Sharing, friendship, truth, and giving freely are the pillars of Cenacolo.

When you enter the Community, you are entrusted to a "guardian angel," a young man who, like you, is on a journey of rebirth. He has already overcome the initial great difficulties and is ready to take care of a new guy who enters shattered and fragmented.

The guardian angel is a brother who follows you like a shadow when you enter the Community, becomes your first friend, explains everything to you, illuminates your first difficult steps, protects you in moments when evil is whispering powerfully in your ear, and helps you to understand the Community rules. He accepts your initial rebelliousness and difficulties with peace and patience. This older brother, always ready to give you a hand at any time of the day or night, is the concrete sign of the love that the Community has for every young man who comes.

The Beginning

The Growth and Expansion

Friendship

Work

Families

Missionary Servants for Love

Consecrated Brothers and Priests

The Missionary Sisters of the Resurrection

The Missions

The Church: Our Home

Biblical Dramas

Festival of Life

Testimonies

Sometimes your guardian angel even annoys you somewhat, because you might feel as if you are not "free," but in reality you discover he is a help to your freedom, which is still weak and fragile in the face of the temptation, memories, and deception of evil.

Being "guarded" and being a "guardian angel" are the two fundamental realities that keep life on its feet: the need to be loved and the need to love. When you enter the Community, you have a great need to be loved, followed, and protected in order to learn to love, to take care of, to protect, and to serve brothers who are weaker. From "guarded" to "guardian," from being loved to choosing to love: this is the Christian journey we travel together each day in order to be reborn to a new life. The young people discover that true healing isn't only not using drugs and not doing evil, but is learning to love, serve, and live goodness faithfully.

God has given me the patience during these years to follow the path He shows me day by day. Slowly the horizon has opened and embraced the many young people in need of love with outstretched arms that desire to embrace the entire world. By now these arms are no longer only mine. There are now, together with mine, the arms of many young people who, after experiencing God's love, have decided to trust Him by giving the love they freely received to those in need.

We are called to be contemplative in two ways . We must have the heart of Mary and the hands of Martha. We have to have calluses on our knees and on our hands. (from the *Rule of Life* of Comunità Cenacolo)

5

The Beautiful Lady

Providence and Its Development

So do not worry and say, "What are we to eat?" or "What are we to drink?" or "What are we to wear?" All these things the pagans seek. Your heavenly Father knows you need them all. But seek first the kingdom [of God] and his righteousness, and all these things will be given you besides. Do not worry about tomorrow; tomorrow will take care of itself. Sufficient for a day is its own evil.

—Matthew 6:31-34

I thought of opening just one house. When one young man would leave, we would just take in another. At a certain point, the motherhouse was overcrowded with mattresses on the floor. The young men continued to arrive. I just couldn't send them away, because they were asking for life, not to eat or to sleep, but to be able to live! They wanted to be saved!

Thinking back, it makes me laugh, because we found the house searching through the Yellow Pages! We were so inexperienced! We found a house in the countryside of Savigliano, seven miles from Saluzzo.

They told us later that the house was valued at fifteen thousand euros, but at the time we purchased it, they asked us for much more. We were a little naïve. The money arrived, however, and we gave it to them.

I have always thought that money serves life and that life is worth much more than money. I also believe that the Lord has blessed us because He sees that we are not attached to money, that we love the life of the young people more than any other thing, more than ourselves.

Even from the beginning, we never wished to accept or ask for money from the State. We have always respected and collaborated with public institutions; but I always believed that a drug addict is not physically sick, even though he might become so later as a consequence of his drug use. Above all, he is sick for hope, sick for love, sick for coherency. He is sick in the soul, one who has lost his way, needing someone to help him find and earn life again with dignity through hard work.

I asked myself if it would be right to ask parents to pay a small monthly fee. But how could one ask for money from desperate and drained families? I said to myself, "No!" I presented this challenge to the Lord: "You are Father, and I have met You in Your splendid Fatherhood. I'll go where You want and do what You want, Your will, in every moment You reveal it to me; but You show Your children the kind of Father You are!" He has never disappointed us. He has always preceded and accompanied us. It has always been like this.

Divine Providence has never made us wait. *Lord, through small and great acts of love of good people, who believe in life and in our proposals, You have always responded to our needs.*

At the beginning of the Community, I often spoke to the guys about Providence in the small, disheveled dining room in Saluzzo. I always had this image: Providence is a Beautiful Lady with large shoulders and a serene, luminous countenance, who wakes up early in the morning before us, happy to put herself at our service, working until evening. Like a good mother, she waits for the last of her children to fall asleep in her arms and only then goes to rest a little herself. I recall the guys listening to me speak of this Beautiful Lady with their eyes wide open, as if desiring to see her.

They understood later that the Beautiful Lady is the "maternity" of God, the beauty of God's maternal face, fascinating and luminous, that tenderly inclines itself toward us, taking care of His children. In all these years, I can testify that this Beautiful Lady, Providence, has never once been late for an appointment.

Providence is unpredictable but dependable; it brings you the essential, and leaves you happy with whatever God provides. We don't ever demand jam in the morning. We are grateful for even a little milk, but if there is no milk, we make tea.

The young people have never complained. They have eaten bread and apples like us. They never expected anything, because basically—and they make us understand it through their peaceful conduct—their desire is to gain back their lives, to give meaning to their lives, and to believe in life again.

I also thank Divine Providence for permitting us to live some extraordinary experiences. The guys have often touched the Fatherhood of God through Providence. By coming to know the living God, who sees and provides for His children, they learn to entrust themselves to Him.

The number of young men grew day by day, and we continued to open houses, first in Italy and then abroad. I remember one year—I no longer recall which—we opened six houses.

It was a joy but also a responsibility. Little by little, as new guys arrived, we understood that our words and actions needed to be more consistent, because they didn't listen to us with their ears; they watched us. They followed us with their eyes, observing everything we did. These young men taught us about "concrete" love and service. The poor called us back to internal and external congruency, to a living faith, and an incarnate word.

For me, living the Christian life of the Gospel—this beautiful story that envelops the entire world—is concreteness, incarnation. This kind of faith does not make you say, "Faith? I don't see faith."

No! No! It's a concrete faith, a life in truth, a dynamism born in you that changes you interiorly before you reflect it exteriorly. Each morning, together with our young people, we encounter

Jesus of Nazareth in the reading of the Word, and in the search for Love, true friendship, mutual forgiveness, a sincere embrace, and reciprocal service. Ours is a beautiful life, because living the faith makes life more beautiful! Faith always amazes us, marvels us, and rouses us to do what we say and propose.

Another Beautiful Lady who has always had a special love for us is Mary. Throughout the years, she has always shown us that she is a faithful Mother. She has taken us to places blessed by her presence, where our young people discover more intensely the gift of prayer and their wounds heal under her tender glance. Mary's silent but living presence in our houses makes something new flourish every day. With her, a more beautiful, bright, and fragrant flower blossoms each day.

One of the most significant Marian moments was the experience we lived during the summer of 1986. Some friends were going to Medjugorje, and they invited me. I didn't know it existed, much less what it was. They said, "Look, Elvira, there is a small town in Bosnia Herzegovina" — a name I didn't even know how to pronounce — "where they say Our Lady is appearing." I was hesitant because I have always been a woman of service with my feet on the ground, not a woman of ecstasies; but because of their insistence, I went. There at Medjugorje, I breathed deeply a simple, authentic faith.

Whenever I experience beautiful things, I always want the young men to experience them too, so I wanted them to touch this faith that could enrich them. I saw that in this small town, with so much poverty, people welcomed everyone and freely gave to one another, expecting nothing in return. I became enthusiastic, thinking, "We live like this, too."

I wanted the young men to see that we weren't the only community that welcomed people without cost, just because a nun started it, but that there were other good, courageous people in the world who love their neighbor.

Some friends who knew my desires paid our bus fare. I told the guys, "Let's go on a pilgrimage! Yes, let's go." So we departed.

We found ourselves in this little town where there were a few hens, a lot of sheep, tobacco fields, and, above all, simple, serene people. The families welcomed us into their homes without asking for anything.

The first time, we stayed for eight days, but then, after a little time, we returned. This second time, in order to avoid splitting up the boys, we brought some tents. We experienced some discomforts and difficulties, but we remained there for forty days. Communism still existed then, and often the police came. "Who are you? We don't want you here! You need to leave!" I looked at him and said, "Yes, Yes! I don't understand; I'm Italian," so we did not move.

Little by little, we began to understand one another, and they asked me, "Who are these guys?" "They are young men who are seeking a true life, and we have come here because Our Lady comes here!"

They answered back, "No Blessed Mother comes here!" At times they picked me up and took me to the police station, holding me for hours while I responded to their questions. After they checked my documents, they would let me go. Although they would pick me up in a car, sometimes I had to walk back in the hot sun to where we had set up our tents. When I arrived, the guys would meet me looking a bit alarmed, but after a glance and a smile, they understood that we could go forward without fear.

Our Lady was there with us! She was definitely there with us! At the beginning, I said it because other people said it, but later I experienced it personally in a simple, concrete way. I noticed that the guys were more serene there, more peaceful. They prayed better, and their deep wounds were healed sooner.

During the following years, we would return again and remain for several months, bringing the tents. We helped the locals by working in their fields and enlarging their houses, so that they could take in pilgrims. Then, one day, three Italians said to me: "Elvira, look, this stretch of land where you set up your tents is for sale. We'll buy it for you!" Providence wanted us there, and I was very happy about it.

Today, our Community house stands where the tents were once pitched. The young men remained there during the war years. Amid countless sacrifices they built it, one stone after the other. Today that house hosts more than a hundred young men of various nationalities, who are welcomed into a great family that breathes peace, smiles, serenity, and true friendship.

The work of God is born in silence. The great, important, and truly useful things for life and eternity are not heard. They don't make any noise. This is how our presence began in that blessed land: in silence, sacrifice, hard work, and the courage to remain steadfast in the midst of a thousand struggles and fears, joyfully walking under the gaze of Mary.

From Medjugorje, a good part of our story spread to other parts of the world. The pilgrims who arrived there came from different countries and encountered the Community, listening to the testimonies of our young people. They were touched and fascinated by what they saw and heard. Some of them returned home with the desire to bring the same seeds of hope to their own lands. Thus, our houses multiplied in various countries of Europe and the world.

From time to time, my collaborators came to me, saying, "Elvira, let's open a mission in Peru ... then a new house in

Argentina.... Let's put up a house at Fatima. Elvira, finally we are in Africa, in Liberia ..." Sometimes I would look at them, stunned and amazed, and ask them where some of these places are.

Those who know me understand that I have never planned anything in my mind, that I've never expected to understand God's plan. The more this story develops, I must admit, the less I understand.

My desire is not to understand but rather to live the will of God, and to be totally open to Him! I want to allow God to fulfill His will, without demanding to know it even a second before He does it.

Thus, each time that we leave for a new land, we ask ourselves: "What will happen? How will they receive us?" There are so many questions and maybe a little bit of human fear when we open a new house. However, we always want to replace that fear with faith. We want to believe in the love of God and the Virgin Mary. We proceed with the peaceful certainty that God will provide!

Some aspects of our Community were born directly from the heart and desires of the guys themselves. There was a period in which I often spoke to them of the importance of meeting and knowing how to choose the right woman in life. I would say to them, "If you had known a true woman, a strong woman, a woman who knew how to teach you about the noes of life, then you would not have taken drugs." I have always been convinced that it is the woman who "makes" the man.

One day, at the end of a long talk, a tall, timid boy approached me. He said to me, "Elvira, you always speak to us about the importance of the woman, but outside no one tells women these things. Who teaches the women how they ought to be? Why don't you do something for them also?"

The Lord always speaks to me through the lives of our guys. I've always listened to their hearts, which are enlightened by God. At that moment, I knew that I had to open a house for women.

A few months later, Providence confirmed this step. Three young women, who had never used drugs, volunteered to receive the girls who came to the meetings asking for help. They left everything, including their jobs. The Holy Spirit gave them the courage!

Before opening a house, it was always necessary for someone to open his heart to God and His plan. True Providence is life and people, not walls. Thus was born the first house for women, from which many others developed. Today we see the fruit of that first "yes." How beautiful it is to contemplate the work of God. How beautiful to see women rise from death to life. The development of the Community marched forward precisely like this!

We opened one house after the other, and then I stopped counting.

In all our Community houses, we live the wonder of seeing young people from so many lands living together, getting along, and forgiving one another. Because they pray together, each day they begin their journey of rebirth in peace.

The Lord has made our Community a sign of His mercy. Throughout the world, the Community proclaims this message: "The mercy of God is infinite."

> As Community we are called to be a small, but luminous sign of hope in today's world of darkness. Our houses should be places where we walk from despair to hope, where those who are disheartened, lonely, sad, marginalized, or in darkness rediscover the light and will to live. (from the *Rule of Life* of Comunità Cenacolo)

6

Children of the Same Womb

Many and Diverse Calls of Life

Without cost you have received;
without cost you are to give.

—Matthew 10:8

The gift of life has been given to us without cost. The first vocation every man is called to live is to welcome life as a gift from the love of God. When we open our eyes in the morning and realize we are alive, we should smile and embrace life. When I say this, I'm asked, "But, whom do I smile at? Whom should I embrace? My husband is at work. The children are still sleeping. It's only me; there is no one with me." I respond, "But are you 'no one'? You must smile at yourself, at your life. You should embrace yourself. You must accept each day happily, loving yourself, your being and existence."

Let us learn to say to ourselves, to our just-awakened life, "Life, I accept you. My life, I embrace you. I smile at you. Today I want to live giving myself. I don't want to be a cadaver anymore!"

I ask the young sisters of the Community to sing this refrain as soon as they wake up, so that they'll hold hands with life every day: "Rise, my friend. Rise, my sister. Rise, rise, my spouse and come." The life that is a friend, a sister, a spouse, a mother ... that life is everything.

Life, which is a gift from God, must be given to others in order to be happy. I often tell the young people that a life that is not given is a life wasted. Today, I decide that what I want to do and should do in my life is love.

Love is the secret of every life reborn and the different callings of life born from the maternal womb of the Cenacolo.

I have never wanted to identify the Community as a place to cure drug addicts or to define it as therapeutic; but rather as a family that welcomes life. We are not interested in the problems of the new arrival, not even his religion, or whether he believes or does not believe. The living person interests us, the person who is suffering and asking for help.

The Community is a mother who accepts the life of her children and opens a path toward the heart of God. She welcomes the life of young people who knock at the door with deep wounds caused by years of addiction, needy of a long journey of healing and formation in the beauty of life.

The Community is open to those who ask to spend some time with us in order to find themselves, even if the world considers them successful. It exists as a place of prayer and service where one is able to discover God's call. It opens its arms to the men and women who feel the burden of their failure and who need a respite that will give them the momentum to begin again.

We ask those who want to be accepted by our community, for whatever reason, to take the time to get to know us, simply to see if our way of life is the answer to their needs or can help their problems.

In our story, the Lord chose the guys themselves from the beginning as workers in His vineyard and first missionaries. Initially, after three years with us, we gave them our blessing and sent them on their way; but some of them said to us, "Elvira, I want to stay. I want to give back what I have received." Some say, "I need to stay longer. I want to grow stronger in what is good." Then another said, "It is not enough for me to be healed. I want to learn to love, to give a little of my life to those who are desperate and ask for help." Therefore, after rebuilding their own lives, some chose to remain in order to give back what they themselves had received, lending a hand to the needs of Community.

The young men who were resurrected were the first missionaries of Cenacolo, who said, "yes." We launched a new project. We call them "missionaries of love," in order to highlight the strength that springs from a free choice of those who decide, for love, to serve those who knock at our door. There are many who give years, and some who give all their life, to the Community's charitable work. Even from the beginning I had a strong intuitive feeling that these young people could give joy and hope, and renew trust in so many discouraged persons. Thus, they become witnesses of God's light and mercy.

As a response to this heartfelt need to sensitize and reawaken the world of troubled youth, and to testify that evil and drugs do not have the last word, the young people themselves created a show, which they named *From the Darkness to the Light*. Through the various performing arts: dance, music, testimonies, songs, and set design—all created by them—they relate the miracle of their rebirth and share the beauty of a reclaimed life lived in the light and truth. Other biblical plays and dramas were born, all of which they brought to the public squares and churches of Europe and the world, giving testimony to the greatness of the Lord's mercy and joy in the faith.

All of this was born from the young people's creativity and sacrifice, as well as a serious, faithful commitment to spend countless hours in rehearsals, in reading of the Word of God, in choreography, and also in practical tasks such as lighting, mounting, and dismantling the stage. At times they sacrificed sleep, sports, and free time; but then beautiful things are always built on sacrifice, which makes them true.

This artistic dimension of song, dance, and theater can be considered one of our Community's apostolates, which testifies to the joy of the faith. It announces to those we meet that Jesus has conquered death, our death! It proclaims that God's last word is not death, but Resurrection! Before each show, I always say that our young men and women on stage are not actors. They are among the "resurrected." They were dead people whom God's love resurrected.

They were youth lost on the street, capable of dancing and speaking of themselves only when they were high or drunk, and now they are capable of doing it with a clean heart and luminous eyes, conquering fears and overcoming timidity. For this reason, our plays are not theater but real deeds and miracles that have happened in us. It is the story of Jesus, who came to save us, which continues to reach us today.

We testify that we have been saved by the blood of a young man, Jesus of Nazareth, the living face of God, who paid for our freedom, giving His last drop of blood for us to reveal how precious we are in the eyes of God. We are His sons and daughters! Each time we are called to witness, we realize that when faith is given and shared, it is strengthened in us.

Some young people dreamed of fulfilling their vocation of family within the Community, so that they can live their engagement and marriage in an authentic life. Thus began the "novitiate of the couple," a concrete verification of love for those who, developing a friendship that is pure and sincere, matured into the vocation of a Christian family.

From this novitiate came the first "Cenacolo couples" or missionary families, to which were added other couples in love with the simple, concrete lifestyle of the Cenacolo.

Some of the couples who marry decide to live their first few years of marriage and family life in Cenacolo, in order to create a solid foundation through the lifestyle and prayer that we live in our Community houses. There are other couples who feel that their vocation is to remain permanently within the Community, fulfilling their answer to God's call by giving themselves fully and freely in service to the youth and children whom they welcome in obedience to the needs of the Community. Abandoning themselves in trust to Divine Providence, they cooperate in the responsibilities of the house and the mission, participating in the moments of prayer, work, and dialogue. These couples form their children in simplicity and the true essentials of life. They are families open to life, with the door of their homes and hearts opened wide to the needs of others. Their presence, along with that of their children, is a strong testimony to the beauty of living the vocation of the Christian life. It is a source of joy and hope for so many youth and children who no longer believe in the value of family.

I am truly stunned by the fact that so many young men and women are becoming missionaries, because all this was not born or programmed by me; rather, God has stirred it up in their hearts, and I have accepted it with joy. My only desire is to allow the Lord to continue to stir up many young people through holy, clean intuitions and to give them the courage to follow the path to God.

For example, our missions were born from the heart of a young man, Nicola, who came to the Community wounded and disappointed by the world of adults. He believed in life right up to the end of his own. He wanted and desired to live it every day for others. His difficult childhood caused him to love children tremendously, especially the abandoned, and to insist that the Community would open its arms to them also.

After encountering the mercy of God and forgiving his father, by whom he had been deeply wounded since early childhood, he felt a strong need to do something for the children who suffer in the world because of the selfishness of adults.

Often he would say to me, "Elvira, if as a child I had discovered that God is the Father and that forgiveness is the true victory over evil—if someone had taught me this and helped me to experience it back then—I would have done much less harm to myself, my family, and society." Often he said to me that if he had been healed, he would have dedicated his life to the children of the streets of Brazil. It was his great dream! He wanted to help these children discover that their lives are a gift from God, in spite of the refusal and wounds of adults. His suffering, offered for this intention until the moment of his holy death, generated our missions for the children of the streets.

Our missions in South America and Africa have grown more than ever. Our consecrated religious brothers and sisters, as well as lay men and women, have given their lives gratuitously by loving, serving, educating, and helping these children so that they can discover and live the beauty of life.

It is precious to see how those who have been saved by Love are capable of helping others to believe in salvation! Thus, Nicola's dream became a reality thanks to his serene but tenacious insistence, his faithful prayer, and his heroic suffering until death, offered for this new birth that the Community felt called to live.

In the Cenacolo's great family, even from the beginning, there was also a place for the parents to be involved in the rediscovery of the faith. Their cross was transformed into help and hope offered to other families marked by the same suffering.

There are also many friends connected to our journey. They met us in different places and situations. Although not touched directly by problems of addictions, their encounter with the Community reenergized their faith and their lives. Many say to me, "Elvira, I realize that I, too, am an addict; I am addicted to my career, to my ambitions, money, work, and my image. I need to change. If your young men and women can do it, so can I."

I rejoice when I see big shots in the world, due to their roles and professional responsibilities, feel comfortable with our guys and girls. They become like children again and find peace with themselves among those who are interested not in their accomplishments but in who they are, among those who do not look at their image but draw truth from their hearts.

Their friendship with us on this journey is greater than everything they do and generously donate to us. A friendship born in faith is truly a precious treasure!

I thought everything that could have been born in the Community had already happened: the guys and girls, couples, parents, friends, missionaries, and children. When some young men and women told me that they wanted to become consecrated in our Community, I was a little hesitant, and I thought, "How can we do this?" I must confess that I did not exult at that moment, but I do now. I dived into the life that the Lord gave me, a life that was already full and passionate, and they came to ask me to take an extra step. Actually, it was not they who came; the Lord sent them. Thus, from the poverty of drug addicts and from this mountain of wreckage, a shoot sprouted: the consecrated life. This was a great surprise from the Holy Spirit and Our Lady.

We have seen and continue to see miracles: young people who want to live the spirit of Comunità Cenacolo in gratuitous and generous service, as a total gift of their lives. First, some young men asked me. Then, after some time, several young women asked if they could consecrate themselves to the Lord through this work. Today those guys and girls are men and women capable of suffering, capable of giving their lives without complaining. Giving joy, love, and sacrifice, they are a great treasure. The consecrated brothers and sisters are the pillars who support the Community. They are the heart of Cenacolo.

The last surprise regarding this work of the Holy Spirit occurred on March 25, 2010, on the solemnity of the Annunciation. The Missionary Sisters of the Resurrection was recognized as a religious institute of diocesan right by the bishop, born in the heart of Comunità Cenacolo, but with a specific call and mission. The life of our consecrated sisters recognized its own identity more clearly. This gave a name and identity to our sisters, called to the vocation to live the primacy of prayer, contemplation, and time listening to God's word, to then "run" in service of wounded man today and reveal to him the mercy of the Father. The Hour of Mercy, 3:00 p.m., constitutes a strong moment of their daily prayer, as they kneel in Eucharistic adoration at the feet of Jesus to implore His Divine Mercy for our work and the whole world, so wounded and lacerated by evil.

The Lord wishes that Comunità Cenacolo's great family live together, keeping in mind that the source of all we are is the same; we are children of the same womb, fruit born of the same tree. When something beautiful rises in the heart of one of the young people, they come to me in trust to share it. I am well aware that it is my duty. I must and want to do this with everything I have: to be the heart, the voice, and the presence that stirs the conscience of the guys and girls. I have nothing to brag about, however; nothing is done out of a sense of duty or against one's will. It is as though a revolution of love exploded, and everything was born and developed day by day without prior reflection, planning, or calculations. Like a peaceful river, it began and continues to flow its course.

You are a son or daughter forever, and you remain so forever. You can live anywhere in the world, choose whatever path for your life, but you always remain a child of the one who gave you light and life. When one arrives at the Community, it's like being reborn in this maternal womb. Each person who enters to become a part of this great family belongs to us in some way, sharing the joys and sorrows, expectations and anxieties, poverty and riches, wretchedness and gifts, defeats and victories. For this reason, the "sons and daughters" of the Community—this is how those who lived with us for years but now live outside the Community define themselves—continue to call and visit whenever they can, making themselves present. They are here with us.

This bond that was born cannot disappear simply because one lives elsewhere, for it's an interior bond. You remain a son or daughter forever in our hearts. You are the children of those who have given you physical life, that of the body; and you are a son or daughter of the one who has given life to your soul: the faith.

> We shall always be a small family of religious brothers and sisters, of lay people, families, of the poor on a journey with the poor, so that we may testify that every baptized person is a missionary and to make clear that, only from communion with Jesus and through prayer, can true mission be born. (from the *Rule of Life* of Comunità Cenacolo)

7

A Family of the Resurrected

The Community in the Church

For freedom Christ set us free;
so stand firm and do not submit again
to the yoke of slavery.

—Galatians 5:1

The connection between the Community and the Church has been present since the beginning. I am a woman of the Church, a nun, so ours is a journey of Community life founded and rooted in the Christian faith. True friendship, prayer, work, and sacrifice are the steps that bring the young people to the living encounter with Jesus in the Word of God and in the sacraments.

Knowing that we belong in the Church, that we are small, living stones in this great building, gives our young men and women so much security. They often rebelled against the Church. They judged her, according to the thinking of the world, but they feel protected and secure when they come to know her, like children who find their mother.

Depending on the world's false truths and empty promises left them profoundly insecure and in search of a stable foundation. Having listened to so many voices that turned out to be illusions and disappointments makes them desire the encounter with the true Word that fulfills what it says.

Today their security rests on the foundation of the Word of God that the Church proclaims, a way that does not delude and a certainty that does not disappoint: the Word of truth that frees hearts. Newfound faith, hope reborn, and resurrected love that comes back to life in us are rooted here on the solid foundations of the Church, on two thousand years of true, living history. The young people may not know this in their minds, but they feel it in their hearts.

The Providence of God has guided our steps in the Church through a special bond with the Diocese of Saluzzo, where we were born, and with each succeeding bishop: the one who gave the initial blessing to our work; the one who followed our growth with attention, discretion, and a little bit of human fear; the one who watched and welcomed us with joy and wonder, embracing and blessing us, seeing the Community as a gift of God and, therefore, giving us a canonical "face" in the Church; the one who followed the international development of our work and accompanied us on the path toward Vatican recognition, constantly sustaining us with sincere friendship on our journey.

As it happened in the beginning, each new house was blessed by the Church. The various projects always begin in the heart of someone who visits one of our houses and listens to the testimonies of the young people. Those from abroad who are particularly touched by this encounter decide to do something for the youth of their own land.

They begin with prayer groups consisting of people who have the same desire to establish a Community house in their country. They begin to entrust this desire to God. Slowly, they begin to know our journey and spirituality more deeply, as well as the way to serve the young people and help their families. As they encounter persons marked by the cross of addiction, they contact one of our houses in order to place them on the path of redemption. Normally this group of people prays and serves life first; sometimes, their own house materializes. What is of God begins in the heart, not on paper — from within, not outside — and is always blessed by prayer in the time of waiting.

We want to be a silent and discreet presence. We don't want to create a stir or draw publicity. We ask to be able to live our communal life simply, accepting and loving those who ask for help, walking together with them so that they may rediscover the "concreteness" of their Christian faith as the precious treasure of their lives.

Therefore, when we open a new house, we ask to be able to do it in silence without a lot of talk. We believe that Community life lived in harmony, joy, prayer, and work with commitment and discipline has the power to touch and impact the heart much more than words. We want to take actions and not just talk!

When we open a new house, the only gift I ask of the bishop is the presence of the Most Holy Eucharist in our chapel. The hearts of the young people whom we welcome can change only by praying before Jesus, who is there alive and present.

The first young person we wish to accept is Jesus; He is the first guest and friend because He will welcome everyone. The guys and girls know it. The first room we prepare in a new house is the chapel. With Jesus among us, everything changes, and I also am much more at peace knowing that He is present with our young people.

At times, during our daily routine or on festive occasions, the local bishops and other shepherds, who are friends of the Community, visit our houses. They feel particularly in sync with Cenacolo's spirituality, mission, and service, thus making us feel the living embrace and blessing of the Church.

Pilgrimages to Lourdes, Medjugorje, Fatima, Czestochowa, and other lands touched by Mary are also deeply significant on their path of healing and faith and are profound experiences for our young men and women and their parents. In these places, one breathes deeply the universality of the Church. We have had the grace of establishing our presence near some of these Marian sites. Our Lady brought us to various lands blessed by her presence, for she knows that they are places of special grace and intense, true experiences of God, places of living mercy.

I am happy when our young people participate in important and powerful moments in the life of the universal Church. For them, it is a new and enriching experience. They see that there is a world out there that believes, that so many other young people desire good, that God is also there outside the Community, and that prayer is not only therapy for drug addicts, but the path to be happy.

On various occasions, we were asked to give our simple testimonies, and this is a gift for us as well as for the ones who listen. Witnessing does us good. It reminds us of the good we have received. It makes us recall who we were before the encounter with the Lord and who we are today. We never want to forget how the mercy of the Lord has transformed us.

Our bond with the Church and the encounters I have had with popes are precious to me. I have always shared my love for the Pope and the Church with the young men and women. The Church is the house of God, where a person who is alone and disheartened finds shelter, refuge, and a family.

I am certain that Peter remained on this earth in the person of the Pope. Anyone who has not been near him, even only once, can't understand the luminous mystery of this living Presence that dwells in him. When you are near him, whether it is Pope John Paul II, Pope Benedict XVI, or Pope Francis, you feel that Peter is alive, that in him abides the tenderness of God, the beauty of the Rock who remains, who gives you security. There you feel a presence that is not only earthly, that isn't only a moment in history, something that is beyond that which you see. It is Someone else who dwells in that person that you encounter. It is Peter, who continues to guide us to the encounter with the Master.

I had various encounters with Pope John Paul II, who always blessed and encouraged us. I especially remember my first meeting with him in July 1990, some days after the seventh birthday of our Community. I was at the Valle d'Aosta with some friends, along the mountain path where the Holy Father would pass, because he was there on vacation. When the Pope was near us, my friends began to cry out — I do not know why — "Sister Elvira is with us." The Holy Father turned, as if looking for me, and asked, "Where from?" They responded in chorus, "From Saluzzo." The Pope, however, did not want everyone's response, only mine; and he continued to look at me deeply, in an indescribable way. Three times he asked, "Where are you from?" I could not speak, but finally I said, "I am from Saluzzo, and I live with the drug addicts." The Pope fixed his eyes on me, and between us, I perceived a profound understanding. Then he blessed my forehead, as if to say to me, "The Church blesses you!" My heart was filled with joy!

I felt also felt great emotion on the various occasions I encountered Pope Benedict XVI. I recall one time in particular. We had gone to Rome on a pilgrimage with many of our young people, and we participated in the Wednesday afternoon audience. I was near a barrier where the Pope would pass. When he came, we looked at each other intensely. He was very serene and not at all in a hurry. He took my hand, and I said to him, "Your Holiness, thank you, because you mentioned and blessed Cenacolo in a special way." He looked at me and said: "Ah, you are the ones!" and he smiled tenderly. Afterward, we looked at each other again, squeezing each other's hand tightly, and I said, " Your Holiness, we are with you. Do not be afraid!"

I met Pope Benedict on various occasions, and we always took each other's hand, looking intensely at each other, speaking the silence of the heart with so much interior friendship. It filled me with tenderness to see and listen to him, for he is a good, humble man. I don't feel that he is not there anymore: he is still there! He is still there!

Today, after all this time, I am more grateful and in love with the Church, and grateful for who she is: strong in ideals, a light that illuminates the path and orients the choices of every man, service to the poor, and bread broken for those who suffer. She is security for everyone.

The Church is young thanks to so many who give their lives and their blood day after day. They find their courage and fidelity in the Eucharistic Communion, in the living encounter with the crucified and risen body of Christ.

The Apostles experienced this. They followed Jesus, and after Pentecost, they began to proclaim Him to everyone from the Cenacle. Thus, the Church was born.

On the journey during these two thousand years of history, men and women of every language, race, and culture have been fascinated by the living encounter with Jesus and have brought His light to the ends of the earth. They have been the Church that brings the Bread of Life to everyone; today I, you, and we are this Church!

> Unity is built on the truth of relationships that are born from the freedom of the heart. The truth in charity is love. To be true with oneself and with others is to be free, clean and humble. Without truth in charity, we can live together, but there is no true unity. (from the *Rule of Life* of Comunità Cenacolo)

In Order to Embrace Humanity!

I have never made plans for the future, but I want to open the door of my heart more and more, the door of love, to embrace all humanity and to welcome those who are still lost and alone. I know that what I have said seems easy, but in reality it is possible only with a miracle from God. I recognize very well my human limitations, my poverties in loving and totally giving myself, but I am also aware that many men and women through the ages allowed themselves to be caught up in the whirlwind of Christ's love, pouring themselves out for others, and I want to be one of them in all my simplicity and fragility.

I feel privileged because it is already a gift to live the possibility of love today, to have a family with whom you can share the richness of life. We couldn't ask for anything more! So many young people have joined their lives to mine, to allow the embrace of God's love to expand their hearts, staying longer in Community to make so many wounded hearts feel loved.

Embracing our brother, we learn to be more human, more in love with Love.

Love ... Love is life.

Love is concreteness.

Love is sacrifice.

Love is humiliation.

Love is hunger at times, but it is always Love.

You must distribute it to everyone, repeating to yourself, "I must love! I want to love!" Because God is love.

We have chosen God. Have we chosen Him? In truth, it is He who has chosen us. We are extremely happy to have met Him; we have believed.

To believe means to love. To love means to act. To act means to serve.

The plan, the only and perennial plan, is to love, love, love ... and serve life with Mary, following the Holy Spirit with love and trust, wherever He desires to take us. This is our life. This is our story.

Decree of Recognition

Rome, October 16, 2009

Dear Friends of Comunità Cenacolo, how can we
not recognize your Community, present by now in
different countries of the world, that inn in which the
wounds of body and soul of many lost persons find
healing, especially young men and women who have lost
the meaning of their lives and the Fatherhood of God?

—His Eminence Cardinal Stanislaw Ryłko,
President of the Pontifical Council for the Laity

On October 16, 2009, the Pontifical Council for the Laity, a Vatican Dicastery, granted the Decree of Recognition to Comunità Cenacolo, which bears the significant date of July 16, 2009.

At the beginning of the twenty-sixth year of the life of the Community, we were confirmed and blessed in our mission by the Church, our Mother and Teacher. It was a profoundly significant moment in our story.

Being welcomed and "embraced" by the heart of the Church, in addition to being an immense joy for Mother Elvira, has been the even more evident certainty that what was born from her "yes" is not a work of "hers" but is the work of the hand of God.

We believe that the inspired words of the Decree, and those spoken by Mother Elvira in a moving and spontaneous way on that occasion, are the most appropriate to express that we are in the Church, which is our identity and our mission.

Decree of Recognition of Comunità Cenacolo
as a Private International Association of the Faithful

The Comunità Cenacolo was born July 16, 1983, through the initiative of Ms. Rita Petrozzi, also known as Mother Elvira, who after some years of waiting and prayer—during which she perceives the call of the Lord to dedicate her life to lonely and marginalized drug addicts—opens the first house of Cenacolo, a dilapidated house on the hill of Saluzzo (CN), where she welcomes the disadvantaged young men of the streets. The profound intuition that guides her is born from the perception that these youth seek, not something, but Someone: the face of the Father. This conviction urged her, not only to offer the many people who knock on the door of the Community a place of recuperation and social service, but also to propose to them an explicit journey of conversion and of rebirth in the faith in the light of Christ.

As stated in the Statute: "The Community wants to be a living sign of God's love and mercy for the poor in a total and gratuitous sharing of life, respectful of the dignity of the person, docile to the voice of the Holy Spirit, abandoned to Divine Providence, attentive to the needs of historical moment" (Article 2).

The Community lives this charism, fostering the personal sanctification of its members and promoting initiatives and works directed toward welcome, the formation and assistance of those who are lost and addicted to drugs.

On March 30, 1998, Comunità Cenacolo was recognized as a Diocesan Association of the Faithful by His Excellency Bishop Diego Natale Bona. This approval was definitively confirmed on December 8, 2005, by his successor His Excellency Bishop Giuseppe Guerrini.

Through the years, numerous people have chosen to commit themselves to this missionary service, opening new houses, activating many works of welcome throughout the world.

On the occasion of the jubilee pilgrimage of the entire Comunità Cenacolo to Rome on February 16, 2000, the Holy Father, John Paul II, wanted to give a lively encouragement to the commitment of its members, affirming: "The Pope is with you, dearest ones. He appreciates your work, and he follows you with his prayer. Do not be afraid or discouraged in the face of difficulties. May the Cross sustain you, and from Christ, who died and is risen, may the constant stimulation come to you to persevere in the walk that you have undertaken, so that you may be testimonies of hope in society."[1]

The Second Vatican Council, as well as the post-conciliar Magisterium, have given special attention to the communal forms of participation in the life of the Church, manifesting toward them a profound esteem and consideration.[2]

In the same way, Pope Saint John Paul II wanted to emphasize the importance of: "promoting the various communal realities which, both in the more traditional and in the newer forms of ecclesial movements, continue to give the Church a vitality that is a gift of God and constitutes an authentic springtime of the Spirit."[3]

Benedict XVI also affirmed that ecclesial movements and new communities "are a gift of the Lord, a precious resource to enrich the entire Christian community with their charisms."[4]

For all of the above,

Given the request made by Ms. Rita Petrozzi, as Foundress and President of Comunità Cenacolo, she urges this Dicastery the juridical recognition of the aforementioned aggregation as a

---

[1] General Audience, in *Teachings of John Paul II*, XXIII, 1, 2000, p. 200.

[2] Decree on the Apostolate of the Laity *Apostolicam actuositatem*, 18, 19, 21; Post-Synodal Apostolic Exhortation *Christifideles laici*, no. 29.

[3] Apostolic Letter *Novo millennio ineunte*, no. 46.

[4] Discourse for participants at a seminar for bishops promoted by the Pontifical Council for the Laity, May 17, 2008, found in *Teachings of Benedict XVI*, IV, 1, 2008, p. 811.

private international association of the faithful and the approval of its Statute;

In consideration of the commendatory letters of the Bishops who testify to the firm faith of the members of the Community, the lively sense of ecclesial communion, as well as the apostolic zeal;

Expected the spread of the Community in various countries of the world;

Considering it appropriate to recognize Comunità Cenacolo and to approve its Statute, and having accepted the remarks made by this Dicastery;

Given the Article 134 of the Apostolic Constitution *Pastor bonus* of the Roman Curia, and canon 322 of the Code of Canon Law, the Pontifical Council for the Laity decrees:

1: The recognition of Comunità Cenacolo as a private international association of the faithful, with legal status, according to canons 298-311 and 321-329 of the Code of Canon Law.

2: The approval of the Statute of the aforementioned aggregation duly authenticated by the Dicastery and deposited in its archives, for an *ad experimentum* period of five years.

Given in the Vatican, 16 July 2009, feast of the Blessed Virgin Mary of Mount Carmel, the twenty-sixth anniversary of the foundation of Comunità Cenacolo.

Signed by
Stanislaw Cardinal Ryłko (President),
Josef Clemons (Secretary)

Intervention of Mother Elvira

"Your Eminence,
Excellencies present Bishops, dear friends:

Words fail to say the wonder, the sincere emotion, and the profound joy of all of us in Comunità Cenacolo for this moment. I am a poor and simple woman whom the Mercy of God has called to reach down to the wounds of today's young people.

I do not have the education nor am I sufficiently cultured for a deep and articulated speech, but I have the great joy of being able to testify truthfully that I am the first to be amazed by what has happened up to now, step by step, in the life of the Community. How could I have invented a story like this? I am the first to contemplate this with so much wonder and the joy to be a living part of this."

In that moment, Mother Elvira put down the sheets of paper with the written speech, and continued spontaneously: "And everything happened without my realizing it. I dove into the Mercy of God. I rolled up my sleeves to love, love, love . . . and serve! Now I ask you to excuse me, but I don't read. Do you know why? Because I don't know how to read. Yes, because when I went to school, I only went to third grade. I had seven brothers and sisters, and often I didn't go at all, so I didn't learn to read. I don't know why the Lord looked upon me . . . but I came to understand that He looked upon me because already from a young age, I had to serve everyone. Everyone had their demands, and I served everyone. And I'm happy! Now Father Stefano will lend me his voice, his heart, and he will continue to read. I can't do it anymore. Is that okay, Your Eminence?

Deeply touched, everyone smiled, and Father Stefano continued reading, saying: "I gladly lend my voice and my heart to Mother Elvira." He began to read the text again.

Truly, as our beloved Pope John Paul II said, "When He intervenes, the Holy Spirit leaves everyone stupefied. Events occur that astound us, radically changing the life of the person and the story." The compassion of God for man drew to serve those young people who play with death in their hearts on the streets and the town squares of their city, unhappy, disillusioned, and deceived by evil and drugs. Their suffering pierced my heart. In prayer, kneeling before the Eucharist, I intensely felt that I could hear—almost physically—their cry of pain, their need for help.

I saw them like "sheep without a shepherd," wandering without direction, although financially secure with money in their pockets, a car, an education, and everything they could want materially . . . yet their hearts filled with sadness and loneliness, lost in an empty life.

I felt within me a push that wasn't my own, that grew more and more. It wasn't my idea or plan. Even I didn't know what was happening, but I felt that I must give those young people something that God had placed inside me for them. I renewed my "yes" to the Lord, patiently waiting for His time.

On July 16, 1983, feast of Our Lady of Mount Carmel, I received from Divine Providence the keys to our first house on the hill of Saluzzo. I thought of opening one house, but with God everything went differently. The young men continued to arrive asking to be reborn. Then we opened another house, then another, first in Italy, then in Europe, and later the missions in Latin America were born. Today, I've lost count.

From the beginning, I wanted to offer the young men a "school of life," where they could rediscover life as a gift from God to be lived in the fullness of His beauty, not just a place of recuperation or social service. I proposed to them what raised me up so many times, giving me trust and hope again: the goodness of the mercy of God, the power of prayer, and total trust in the Providence of God, who has never disappointed me.

On our journey through the years, young people joined me who decided to give their lives to God in order to share the faith in gratuitous service to their neighbor. The number of arms and hearts of those who give their lives in total self-donation of this work multiplied. Thus, the unexpected and unplanned missionary horizon burst open!

Later, families of our young men and women joined us, often profoundly wounded families. However, the mercy of God transformed their failure and desperation into an opportunity for conversion and a new Christian life, open to forgiveness and service.

So many friends, contemplating the miracle of resurrection of our young men and women, rediscovered the joy of the faith as members of the Church and faithfulness to prayer as the power to live their different responsibilities in a Christian way.

Thus, a great family was formed of people reborn through the mercy of God, walking together from the darkness to the light.

What a great gift we live today, seeing this family welcomed, embraced, and blessed by the Church! We can truly proclaim, with the voice of the psalmist, "The Lord raises the needy from the dust, lifts the poor from the ash heap, seats them with princes, the princes of his people (Ps. 113:7-8)."

With profound gratitude, I want to thank the bishops of the Diocese of Saluzzo, where the Providence of God willed the birth of Comunità Cenacolo. They reached down to us in these years with loving guidance.

A special thanks to His Excellency Bishop Bona, who had "God's gaze" on our work, welcoming us into the Church with the first diocesan approval, which took place on the solemnity of Pentecost in 1998, on the same significant day when Pope John Paul II met for the first time with all the Movements and the New Communities in Saint Peter's Square.

A sincere thanks goes then to His Excellency Bishop Guerini, who has always kindly supported our reality, since his arrival into the diocese, by giving it the definitive diocesan approval. From the very beginning, he has fully supported and blessed the journey that brought us today to this recognition as an international association.

An immense thanks then to the Holy Father, who through the Dicastery over which you preside, Your Eminence Cardinal Ryłko, welcomes us into the "heart" of the Universal Church.

The heart of Peter is a good Samaritan that welcomes a Community of the poor, of persons who have experienced the fragility and weakness of the human condition, but who today are happy to be able to testify to everyone that the experience of the mercy of God is stronger than every sin, that the Resurrection of Christ is true victory over death, and that the Christian life is the path to restore dignity and meaning to the life of man.

May the great gesture of love that we receive today with this Decree of Recognition from our Mother and Teacher, the Church, commit us always to be more responsible children who are worthy of this gift. May it help us to develop a convicted, robust faith and make us live a stronger, more authentic bond in prayer, in living testimony, service, and sincere obedience to the Holy Father and his collaborators.

I want to conclude, recalling the words of our Holy Father Benedict XVI, directed at the Movements and New Communities on Pentecost 2006, for I feel they are words especially fitting for us in this moment: "In this world, full of fictitious freedom that destroys the environment and man, we desire with the power of the Holy Spirit, to learn true freedom together, to build schools of freedom, to demonstrate to others through our lives that we are free and how beautiful it is to be truly free in the true freedom of the children of God."

May Comunità Cenacolo always be a greater testimony of this true freedom of the children of God and an expression of the maternal love of the Church, which reaches down to the wounds of man to take care of him, rendering him capable of finding the way home again, the way of the Truth that makes us free.

With Mary's heart of joy, the joy of the Magnificat, entrusting our new path totally to her, we express to you a profound and heartfelt gratitude.

Thank you with all our heart for welcoming us, for listening to us, and for loving us!

God Exists! I Have Met Him!

Catechism of Mother Elvira to the Young People
Medjugorje, August 1998

What was from the beginning,
what we have heard,
what we have seen with our eyes,
what we looked upon
and touched with our hands
concerns the Word of life ...
we proclaim now to you,
so that you too may have
fellowship with us.

—1 John 1:1, 3

We were created by a thought, an act of love. We became the visible and palpable fulfillment of God's dream, and when God dreams, He creates. Each one of us is this dream. We should learn to contemplate this dream of God by looking at one another. I want to give you some terrific news, the most beautiful news, the only true news: "God exists, and I have met Him!"

Young people, close your eyes. The young are all those who have a heart that beats, that vibrates. Young people are all those who have a clean heart, virginal, because it is full of love. Even I, who am over sixty years old, still feel super young. Close your eyes, and cry out with me: "God exists, and I have encountered Him! Let's say it all together!"

Young people, stop being followers! Stop being pagan Christians! Is it true that God exists and that you have met Him? Have you encountered Him in your solitude, your anger, your violence, and your sullenness? Have you met Him in the face of your father, whom you reject because his words don't match his actions? Have you met Him in the possessiveness of your mother, who annoys you?

I have met Him in the marginalization, the darkness, and the cry of my sins. God exists, and I encountered Him precisely when I thought I was crushed, when I failed, and when I was desperate and condemned to death forever. God exists, and I have met Him.

I have encountered Him in the drunkard's face, swollen from hitting the pavement so many times. I met Him in the poor, in the malnourished mother who did not know how she would give milk to her baby. I met Him in the injustice I lived at school and at work. I met Him in the marginalized, in the youth seeking happiness, making holes in his arms with a syringe.

Yes, God exists; He exists in my life story. He exists in my daily life, and I must meet Him in the real events of my life. He exists, and He is a God who speaks. He is a God who addresses me. He wishes to have me connected to Him for the redemption and salvation of all His creatures.

Young people, we possess an immense treasure. Each one of us has encountered God on our present journey. We knew Him when we were on the cross, crying out to Him, "Father, why have you abandoned me?" Yes, God is this Life in life, and He is this life that I live moment to moment. He is the Holy Spirit within us, crying out continuously with indescribable moans, "Abba! Abba! Abba!" Let us unite ourselves to this powerful and delicate voice, this constant voice within that turns toward the Father. Today young people experience the reality of being orphans. They live in solitude and abandonment because they have not encountered a maternal or paternal face, the face of a friend or spouse — the face of love.

God is the love we are always seeking. God is that insatiable love, that never-ending embrace. God is the living hope and trust we want to possess all day and every day of our lives.

The Holy Spirit who dwells in us asks to make us journey, asks each one of us to take possession our lives. Let's not yield even the slightest space to emptiness, doubt, fear, hate, or rancor.

Let us reconcile with one another, so that the Holy Spirit may be able to work in us, live in us, and bring forth the fullness of what we were always seeking.

We must ask ourselves a question: Does joy interest us? Does love interest us? Does happiness interest us? Does life interest us? Do good and well-being interest us? The Holy Spirit is all of this! He is love, joy, hope, happiness, exultation, dance, embraces, fragrance, and flowers. He is the life that gives rebirth to every new day.

You young people seek the truth of life more than we do, and in life it is the Holy Spirit within us that says, "Make room for me! Make room for me!" Each of us knows the spaces that are dedicated to the spirit of this world, the false and deceptive spirit of this world, interested in material things and passing pleasures that leave a bitter taste in the mouth. These pleasures make you feel humiliated, worthless, exploited, and slapped by evil.

Young people, you have said these things. I've learned these things from you. You thought you were keeping them secret, but your presence here to pray and listen to God, to sit in the school of Mary, tells us that you are tired of the falsehood of this world, its hypocrisy, lies, and masks.

You have been saying that you believe in life, love, and hope; but what you are really saying is that you believe in mercy. You are our living and daily theology. We adults must learn to read the open book that you are.

On behalf of your families, the Church, school, and work, and in the name of religious people, priests, nuns, and all those who in the past have disappointed you, I say, "Forgive us!" Forgive our falsity, hypocrisy, and incoherence. Forgive us, and do not accuse us. We cannot be the models that you are seeking. Your parents cannot be the models that you expect to have. None of us can completely fill your heart with truth, coherency, light, peace, and love.

The true model that does not disappoint is another, the One to whom we look and from whom we seek direction every day. He is Jesus, Son of Mary and Son of God. He is Jesus the Crucified One, the victorious Crucified One, and the Resurrected One. He is our model. He is our answer.

Young people, you certainly have the right to demand more from us adults, to point a finger in order to show us our inconsistencies, but we can no longer delude you. We, like you, need forgiveness every day and all day. Believe me, it is so! Each day, with you, we climb the hill of Calvary, because only from the Cross comes the complete, inexhaustible answer to our lives, to my life and to your lives. We must stop deluding ourselves and become concrete in our faith! Our faith began with a Man who was an apparent failure, a dead man hanging on a Cross. He seemed to be a failure, and everyone shook their heads in disappointment. We can't brag about victories we didn't win. Our victory is Jesus, victorious from that Cross! He is risen. He hasn't disappointed us; He hasn't failed. He won with the power of love that gave everything. He conquered with the power of forgiveness until the very end!

Do you know what I was saying to a group of young people in Community the other day? You are all seeking your path in life, and the majority of girls are thinking about a "prince charming," while the guys are seeking the most fascinating, pretty, available, and "easy" girl.

I say to you, before choosing the guy or the girl, first choose what religious order you would enter if the Lord called you to the consecrated life. This is the truth: choose the Cross. The unknown of each choice can be explained solely with the Cross.

Before you choose that guy and make the error of putting your life into his hands forever, choose the Cross. Embrace the Cross, and you will find yourself embraced by Jesus, the Crucified One. Then you can be faithful to that guy. You will be able to become a woman who knows how to serve a man out of love, not a woman forced and obligated to serve him only because he married you.

You will be a servant for love, who gradually comes to feel like a queen; because to serve out of love is the greatest richness, the greatest dignity, the path to become a true queen. No one will ever be able to take this title from you when you begin to wash the dirty feet of everyone out of love and when you no longer fear washing pots and pans out of love! You will be a servant for love! You will feel like a queen because you will dominate your instincts of ambition, habit, and criticism. All this is possible only if you choose the Cross first. If you put your life in the hands of God, if you say "yes" to Him, you can do it.

To you, young guys and men, I say that it is too small-minded to think only, "I want to get married. I like that girl." Love is not only what "I like," but also the will, respect, waiting, sacrifice, and the gift of yourself to the person you love. The "I want to have a beautiful family" is so superficial, at times even banal. We have seen young men who have not challenged themselves. They didn't question themselves. They got married as if it was an adventure, and they ended up alone and sad. Ask yourself if your vocation is truly marriage. Begin asking yourself in the depth of your being, and if you feel that the path prepared for you is to become a husband, then be a gift for your bride. Be a gift for her; she should be a gift for you. In order to live this exchange of gifts forever, you must understand that you are beginning a life in two. It's not just you alone to reason and decide solely with your head, always to have the last word; instead, you should let your wife express her thoughts, sentiments, feelings, and desires. You must not think, "She will make me happy!" but "What should I do to make my wife happy?" Then you will be a mature man, a faithful spouse, a father, capable of loving.

Perhaps many of you fear being called to the consecrated life, to help Jesus embrace and heal the wounds of humanity. You continue going around in circles, trying to find that holy person who will say to you, "Consecrate yourself to God. Be a priest." No! God speaks to the heart. We can advise, confirm, encourage, but not substitute. We have a God who is the way, the truth, and the life. Do you think that He will not indicate the way if you truly wish to know it? First, eliminate your fear of taking a risk, the fear of totally involving yourself, because this is the fear that is obstructing your choice.

In these days, we've spoken about important values much more necessary than the food we eat: the nourishment of prayer. I think of some young people who dedicate time to prayer but always remain doubtful and indecisive. That prayer is only sentiment, ecstasy. What we want to see always seems beyond us. Instead, prayer is a power inside us. It is a movement that makes you courageous and pushes you to act with audacity. Prayer draws you into the will of God. It changes you.

Let us not offend the Lord by avoiding Him. If this God does not speak to you, it is a sign that you are kneeling before an idol. It is not the God of Jesus Christ. If He is not a God that gives you audacity, courage, and the freedom to detach from self, your fears, your complexes, and your sins, and does not bring you into the midst of the world in order to walk and testify, it is not the God of Jesus Christ. You are too comfortable. You have created a ghost of your own making. You have put yourself in prison. If we meet the God of Jesus, He is a God who welcomes you, calls you, fills you, and sends you. He sends you to cry out what we have cried out here, all of us: God exists, and I have encountered Him. Beginning where? From the mission of your home.

God exists, and I have met Him. This God whom you have encountered cannot leave you in that false peace, the peace of the cemeteries that at times reigns in families. He stimulates you and puts fire inside you, because God's great passion is our salvation.

We are all responsible when we say, "I have encountered Him!" We have encountered Him not because we are better and more beautiful but for a precise responsibility. We must cry out to everyone, always. Do you know that an authentic cry that moves people most? It is the scandal of our genuine conversion. When people are aware of it, they immediately go into crisis and begin to observe us more profoundly. A true conversion invites you to make some radical choices, choices that are contrary to the world, choices that amaze and marvel people.

I am speaking above all to you young people. We have to be driven in our faith. Our faith has to be solidified by our concrete choices. We must allow the power of God to work in us. Today the world needs concrete answers, living and eternal answers; and those choices that we make in God are answers that proclaim eternity.

A life will be renewed solely through the Cross. Don't believe it when they give you an alternative. The truth is that our God has sacrificed Himself on the Cross to speak to us of His love and to tell us that happiness is born from the embrace with the Crucified One. The moment of the Cross will come. If we wish to taste happiness and joy, let us prepare for that moment. Let us embrace the Cross of Christ, in order to be able to embrace and carry the crosses of life in faith with Him.

The adventure with God is something that fascinates you, and you remain convinced and sculpted interiorly forever; for God does not call only once. He calls everyone every moment of the day and, while He calls you, He remakes you and rebuilds you. He changes your sadness into joy, your weakness into strength, and your sins into mercy. You cannot resist this God who creates and re-creates you. Woe to me if I am the same as I was yesterday. We walk through His fidelity; we change through His grace.

Today, after all these years, even I can say that I am changed. I am more good. I believe more. I have experienced God's love in a truer way. Yes, God exists, and we have encountered Him.

He is here! He is alive! He walks with us!

I thank you for having listened to me,
and I ask you, please, to pray for us.
We pray for you, with much love.
Thank you.... I embrace all of you.

—Mother Elvira

Resources

Italy

Comunità Cenacolo
Via S. Lorenzo 35
12037 Saluzzo (CN) Italy

website: www.comunitacenacolo.it
phone: 39 0175 46122; fax 39 0175 476369
e-mail: info@comunitacenacolo.it

United States

Comunità Cenacolo America
9485 Regency Square Blvd, Suite 110
Jacksonville, FL 32225

website: HopeReborn.org
phone: 904.501.7872

For information on entering, please contact
a regional Servant of Hope found at:

www.hopereborn.org/to-enter/
servants-of-hope-contact-information/

The EMBRACE *of* GOD'S MERCY

Ireland

Our Lady of Knock House
Knock, County Mayo

website: communitycenacolo.ie
e-mail: info@communitycenacolo.ie
phone: 094 9388286

England

Cenacolo Community UK
Cumbria, LA8 9DH

website: cenacolouk.org
e-mail: cenacolouk@gmail.com
phone: 01539 736222

About the Author

Rita Agnese Petrozzi, known as Mother Elvira, is identified by many as "the drug addicts' nun." She was born at Sora, a province of Frosinone (Lazio), on January 21, 1937. During the Second World War, her poor family immigrated to Alexandria, where she experienced the discomforts and misery of the postwar period, and at home she became the family's "servant." At nineteen, she entered the convent at Borgaro Torinese, with the Sisters of Charity of St. Giovanna Antida Touret and became Sister Elvira. During the mid-seventies she felt a strong calling to dedicate herself to young people; and after a long wait, on July 16, 1983, she founded the Comunità Cenacolo (Community of the Cenacle/Upper Room) at Saluzzo (CN), a place that gives assistance and support, but above all faith, to the youth (and their families) in need of it.

Throughout the years, many young volunteers, families, and consecrated brothers and sisters have joined Mother Elvira in dedicating their lives to the works of the Community. The first ecclesial recognition, at the diocesan level, occurred on Pentecost 1998; then, following the international development of their work, in July 2009, the Community was recognized by the Pontifical Council for the Laity (a Vatican Dicastery), as a Private

International Association of the Faithful. Today, the Community has over seventy houses in eighteen countries where thousands of the needy, in particular young people and babies from the street, are accepted gratis. From the internal organization there has also arisen a religious family, the Missionary Sisters of the Resurrection. Today Mother Elvira lives near the motherhouse of Comunità Cenacolo at Saluzzo and is the person of referral for the entire reality. In a particular way, during the last years, she has dedicated herself more intensely to prayer, to the formation of the young sisters, and to visiting the various houses.